Lighttpd

Installing, compiling, configuring, optimizing, and securing this lightning-fast web server

Andre Bogus

PUBLISHING

BIRMINGHAM - MUMBAI

Lighttpd

First published: October 2008

Production Reference: 1151008

Published by Packt Publishing Ltd.
32 Lincoln Road
Olton
Birmingham, B27 6PA, UK.

ISBN 978-1-847192-10-3

www.packtpub.com

Cover Image by Vinayak Chittar (vinayak.chittar@gmail.com)

Credits

Author

Andre Bogus

Reviewer

Peter Lavetsky

Development Editor

Swapna V. Verlekar

Technical Editors

Dhiraj Chandiramani

Rasika Sathe

Editorial Team Leader

Akshara Aware

Project Manager

Abhijeet Deobhakta

Project Coordinator

Abhijeet Deobhakta

Indexer

Monica Ajmera

Proofreader

Claire Lane

Production Coordinator

Shantanu Zagade

Cover Work

Shantanu Zagade

About the Author

Andre Bogus is a musician turned programmer. He has worked in different jobs from voice acting to programming to teaching to managing software projects. At the moment he works as a consultant and implementer for KOGIT GmbH, an Identity Management company based in Germany.

He found Lighttpd while searching for the ideal software for his personal web server and quickly learned the tricks to make it do what he wanted. He enjoys learning new things and telling others about them. When his full schedule allows it, he can be found on the #lighttpd IRC channel.

He wants to thank his wife, Ania, without whose support he would not have been able to finish this book. Also he appreciates his employer for allowing him to write besides his day job. The nice people at PACKT Publishing have also earned his gratitude by helping this book to become what it is.

About the Reviewer

Peter Lavetsky is a Senior Research and Development Analyst with `Dealer.com`, located in Burlington, VT. He has written multiple Lighttpd plugins as well as tuned many instances tailored to Dealer.com's web serving needs. Peter currently works on integrating third-parties into the `Dealer.com` platform, including Google Base and Google AdWords. In his spare time he enjoys checkraising the turn and feeding the tiger shark.

Table of Contents

Preface

This book explains downloading, installing, and configuring the Lighttpd HTTP server, illustrates how to extend it with modules and Lua code, shows a migration path from Apache httpd, gives case studies in setting up a number of popular web applications, and even demonstrates how to extend Lighttpd by writing our own modules.

The name Lighttpd (pronounced "Lighty") is an abbreviation pulling together Light (as in weight) and HTTPD (which is an abbreviation for Hypertext Transport Protocol Daemon, in short web server). Early versions called themselves LightTPD to emphasize the "lightweight" part, but this led to confusion over pronunciation and meaning, so the capitalization was reduced.

What This Book Covers

Chapter 1 gives directions how to obtain Lighttpd. Regardless, if we want to use a binary package or build from source, everything is there. In addition, dependencies, optional packages, and compilation options are examined. After working through this chapter, we should have an installed Lighttpd to work with.

Chapter 2 introduces all elements of the configuration language by example. Usable examples include sending the correct MIME type, setting up multiple domains, rewriting, and redirecting. Also the command line options are explained. For those who are not fluent in regular expressions, the chapter has an excursion. At the end of this chapter, we have our Lighttpd up and running.

Chapter 3 builds on the concepts of the second chapter and discusses the configuration various CGI-like interfaces, three modules for virtual hosting, also introducing the MySQL database, which is used in one of the modules.

Chapter 4 shows how to set up Lighttpd as a download or streaming server, covering optimizations for large downloads as well as guarding our site against denial of service attacks, dealing with proxies, and restricting download speeds for anonymous clients.

Chapter 5 extends our Lighttpd to learn more about our users: Geo-tracking the location from the client IP address, dissecting the page traversal behavior ("clickstream analysis") and other data points. Also responsible access logging practices are outlined.

Chapter 6 adds SSL support to our Lighttpd and walks through the steps to acquire or create the required certificates, whether we obtain a certificate from a public or corporate certificate authority, self-sign a certificate, or become our own certificate authority.

Chapter 7 helps us securing our Lighttpd by authorizing access, limiting traffic by IP to thwart denial-of-service attacks, and measuring our success by rigorously examination of our log files. Setting up log rotate and log parsers is also covered.

Chapter 8 concerns itself with limiting the potential damage a subverted Lighttpd could do to the system. The techniques to achieve this are reducing privileges and putting the whole Lighttpd in a secluded environment. Containing Lighttpd and a CGI backend in different environments is also demonstrated.

Chapter 9 shows a strategy to optimize our Lighttpd from system and configuration settings to the source code itself. The chapter also shows specific optimizations known to yield benefits across most systems.

Chapter 10 takes a pragmatic look on the migration path from Apache httpd. It shows how to port basic configuration, rewrite and redirect rules, how to deal with `.htaccess` files, and even discusses when not to migrate.

Chapter 11 revisits the CGI interfaces by getting various example applications from Ruby on Rails over WordPress, phpMyAdmin, trac, and AWstats to AjaxTerm up and running with our Lighttpd.

Chapter 12 adds the small and fast scripting language Lua to the mix, which can be used to extend the functionality of Lighttpd by `mod_magnet` or as a backend language by the Lua/FastCGI interface written by the same author as Lighttpd. Both options are discussed, along with an introduction to the language itself.

Chapter 13 gives a run down of extending Lighttpd by extending existing modules or even writing our own. With these modules, we can change the behavior of Lighttpd from request parsing to sending or altering content. This chapter is aimed at an average C programmer.

Appendix A lists the HTTP status codes that our Lighttpd can return on answering a request, giving directions which chapter or other source might have more information on each request.

Appendix B is the module and configuration index. Each configuration option for every Lighttpd module of the official distribution is explained here in one or two short sentences. Forgotten how a configuration option is written, what type it has or what it means? Look no further.

What You Need For this Book

To work through this book effectively, you will need at least a computer running on one of the supported operating systems (Refer to Chapter 1 on installation) connected to the Internet. Basic knowledge about computers, the Internet, (especially the HTTP protocol), and one or more programming language is also helpful.

Who is This Book For

This book pulls together all the information and gives helpful examples instead of complex theories. As Lighttpd is mostly used in an environment, common interfaces are also shown.

So, if you are a web developer or an administrator, and you want to learn how you can install, configure, secure, optimize (or even extend), and generally get the most out of Lighttpd, you should read this book.

Now, before reaping the benefits of Lighttpd, we first need to download and install it.

Conventions

In this book, you will find a number of styles of text that distinguish between different kinds of information. Here are some examples of these styles, and an explanation of their meaning.

Code words in text are shown as follows: "We can include other contexts through the use of the `include` directive."

A block of code will be set as follows:

```
$HTTP["url"] =~ ".py" { # use SCGI for python files
   proxy_core.protocol = "scgi"
   proxy-core.balancer = "carp" # tries to keep processes together
   proxy-core.backends = { # we have 3 SCGI servers to balance:
       "127.0.0.1:3456", # a local port (by IP address)
       "otherhost.mydomain.net:3456", # a port on another host
       "unix:/tmp/python.socket" # a unix socket
   }
   proxy-core.max-pool-size = 3 # for SCGI the number of backends
   # for other options, see Appendix B
}
```

When we wish to draw your attention to a particular part of a code block, the relevant lines or items will be made bold:

```
<startup>

while (FCGI_Accept())
    <handle request>

<cleanup>
```

Any command-line input and output is written as follows:

```
$ gcc -Wall -O2 -g -o magnet magnet.c -lfcgi -llua -lm -ldl -Wl,-E
```

New terms and **important words** are introduced in a bold-type font. Words that you see on the screen, in menus or dialog boxes for example, appear in our text like this: "clicking the **Next** button moves you to the next screen".

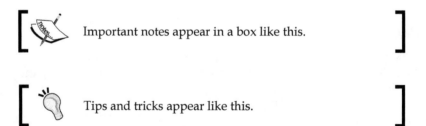

Important notes appear in a box like this.

Tips and tricks appear like this.

Reader Feedback

Feedback from our readers is always welcome. Let us know what you think about this book, what you liked or may have disliked. Reader feedback is important for us to develop titles that you really get the most out of.

To send us general feedback, simply drop an email to feedback@packtpub.com, making sure to mention the book title in the subject of your message.

If there is a book that you need and would like to see us publish, please send us a note in the **SUGGEST A TITLE** form on www.packtpub.com or email suggest@packtpub.com.

If there is a topic that you have expertise in and you are interested in either writing or contributing to a book, see our author guide on www.packtpub.com/authors.

Customer Support

Now that you are the proud owner of a Packt book, we have a number of things to help you to get the most from your purchase.

Downloading the Example Code for the Book

Visit http://www.packtpub.com/files/code/2103_Code.zip to directly download the example code.

The downloadable files contain instructions on how to use them.

Errata

Although we have taken every care to ensure the accuracy of our contents, mistakes do happen. If you find a mistake in one of our books — maybe a mistake in text or code — we would be grateful if you would report this to us. By doing this you can save other readers from frustration, and help to improve subsequent versions of this book. If you find any errata, report them by visiting http://www.packtpub.com/support, selecting your book, clicking on the **let us know** link, and entering the details of your errata. Once your errata are verified, your submission will be accepted and the errata added to the list of existing errata. The existing errata can be viewed by selecting your title from http://www.packtpub.com/support.

Piracy

Piracy of copyright material on the Internet is an ongoing problem across all media. At Packt, we take the protection of our copyright and licenses very seriously. If you come across any illegal copies of our works in any form on the Internet, please provide the location address or website name immediately so we can pursue a remedy.

Please contact us at copyright@packtpub.com with a link to the suspected pirated material.

We appreciate your help in protecting our authors, and our ability to bring you valuable content.

Questions

You can contact us at questions@packtpub.com if you are having a problem with some aspect of the book, and we will do our best to address it.

Introduction to Lighttpd

1

In this chapter, we will learn:

- What Lighttpd is
- How to install Lighttpd
- How to build Lighttpd using:
    - Autotools
    - CMake

What is Lighttpd? Lighttpd, or Lighty, as it is affectionately called, is an extensible, modular, low-footprint, single-threaded, high performance, web server that will happily run on small servers, and outperform an Apache server or Microsoft IIS in most settings. Lighttpd powers many large sites, such as the YouTube video download servers and the image upload server of Wikipedia. At the time of this writing, Lighttpd has the fifth place in the netcraft web server top ten. The plugin architecture encourages developing custom modules and trying new ideas. The development community around Lighttpd is friendly, helpful and pragmatic, and the documentation, though a little scattered, is quite thorough, if you know where to look.

Installing Lighttpd

Lighttpd has very little dependencies considering the wealth of functionalities it provides. For most systems, getting Lighttpd is just a matter of downloading and installing a package. Before we go out and get one, we better know what we want. There are two branches of Lighttpd: a stable branch and a development branch.

The stable branch is very solid and changes at the most once every two months (if bug fixes are not counted, then about once a year), allowing the developers to concentrate on bug fixes. The development branch moves faster, with a new release every four to six weeks. The development snapshots contain new shiny features, but can also contain hidden bugs, break old features and can generally be less stable.

At the time of writing, version 1.4.19 is deemed to be the stable version, while pre-releases of the upcoming 1.5.0 version are distributed for more testing before the final release. Some systems might have packages of older versions, but anything older than the stable branch many contain known security holes.

For a live server, or if we want the latest versions, we usually compile Lighttpd from sources. For a development server, we might take the easy route and install a precompiled package to leave the worries about dependencies to whoever maintains the package database.

The last question is, on which system we should use Lighttpd? My pragmatic advice is to use what you have. For a development system, take the platform you currently work on. For integration and production platforms, this advice needs to be constrained a little—apart from Windows, which allows too little connections to be open in parallel, most operating systems are suitable for production use—the POSIX-implementing ones (Linux, every BSD, Solaris, Mac OS X, and so on) also benefit from numerous optimizations.

Now, without further ado, here is a list of binary packages per system:

System	Download address or command

Debian GNU/Linux, Ubuntu, Knoppix, other Derivatives	`apt-get install libpcre3`
	`apt-get install zlib1g`
	`apt-get install mysql-common libmysqlclient12`
	`apt-get install lighttpd lighttpd-doc`

Fedora / Red Hat Novell / SuSE Linux other RPM-based distributions	`yum install pcre`
	`yum install zlib`
	`wget http://www.kevindustries.com/media/kw/files/`
	`linux/lighttpd/RPMS/lighttpd-1.4.13-3.KWEL4.i386.`
	`rpm rpm -Uhv lighttpd-1.4.13-3.KWEL4.i386.rpm`

Gentoo Linux	`emerge lighttpd`
Windows	`http://www.kevinworthington.com:8181/?cat=20`

To compile Lighttpd from source, download the latest source package from `http://lighttpd.net/download/`. Between Lighttpd versions 1.4.19 and 1.5.0, the build system has changed from Autotools to CMake. Before we can install it, we need the following:

- A compiler and toolchain—most systems have **gcc** make and a **libc** (usually **glibc**) providing the usual functions. For some embedded platforms, the need to define some constants by hand before cross-compiling has been observed.

- PCRE—the **libpcre** package (`http://www.pcre.org`) supplies PERL-compatible regular expressions to Lighttpd. Lighttpd will run without it, but won't do anything more complex than serving web pages directly under only one hostname and path, without any rewriting or redirecting.

Apart from these, there are some optional packages that expand the capabilities of Lighttpd:

- **OpenSSL** (`http://openssl.org`) or any other SSL library (but OpenSSL is the most-tested one) is needed for transport layer encryption, so our site can be accessed via https.

- **zlib** (`http://www.zlib.org`) is required for `mod_compress` to supply on-the-fly gzip compression for static content. As virtually every system has zlib available, this should not concern us.

- **bzip2** (`http://www.bzip.org`) can also be used by `mod_compress` static content for clients who allow bzip2 compression. It is a little slower than zlib, but achieves higher compression rates.

- **Lua** (`http://www.lua.org`) is a small, fast, powerful scripting language, which is a perfect match for Lighttpd and can be embedded as `mod_magnet`.

- **MySQL** (`http://www.mysql.org`) is a product by the company that employs the author of Lighttpd. Therefore, it is no surprise that Lighttpd uses MySQL for database-backed virtual hosting. Also, under Debian, a binary install depends on MySQL.

- **pkg-config** (`http://pkgconfig.freedesktop.org`) is not strictly necessary, but it will make the installation easier. Especially for Lua, the Lighttpd installation process relies on it unless given explicit library paths.

Building Lighttpd using Autotools

Lighttpd was built using Autotools until version 1.5.0, in which the authors experimented with CMake (and other build systems). The Autotools build system has been around for some time. So, almost every system that has a sufficient toolchain can build Lighttpd.

Note that the building can and should be done as a normal user, while the installation must usually be done as a superuser, unless the target directory is owned by the normal user. The easiest way (provided we have **sudo**) is:

```
configure && make && sudo make install
```

Before we enter this command line, we can set a few environment variables that will affect the build process. We can do this in a bash compatible shell using:

```
export SOME_VAR=X
```

This will set the variable SOME_VAR to X and export it to the shell. Alternatively, we can just omit the export if we write the variable declarations at the beginning of our command, as in:

```
SOME_VAR=X; OTHER_VAR=Y; configure
```

Here are the most important variables:

Variable name	Useful value	Description
CC	arm-gcc icc	Specify an alternate compiler if you cross-compile Lighttpd or have a more optimizing compiler compared to gcc.
CFLAGS LDFLAGS	-g -Os -L/usr/local/lib	These options go to the gcc compiler. Read up on gcc for further information.
PKG_CONFIG	/opt/pkg_config	We may need to specify where pkg-config is, if configure cannot find it.
FAM_CFLAGS FAM_LIBS	-I/opt/fam/include -L/opt/fam/lib	We can specify alternate C Flags and linker settings (for example, paths) for FAM.
LUA_CFLAGS LUA_LIBS	-I/usr/include/lua/ -llua	This tells configure where to find Lua (for example, if pkg-config is missing)

configure takes some options to select features. These options are usually expressed as:

```
configure --with-lua=/usr/src/lua-5.1 --with-pcre
```

Note that for every "with-something" option, there also is a "without-something" option that does the exact opposite. Here are the most important options:

Parameter (example)	Description
--help	This makes configure print a help screen and exit.
--prefix=/usr/ --prefix=/opt/lighttpd/	Specify your installation directory if you want to install Lighttpd at a location different from `default/usr/local/`.
--bindir=... --sbindir=... --datadir=... --libdir=... --sysconfdir=...	We can also set each directory individually for the installation process.
--host=PLATFORM --target=PLATFORM --build=PLATFORM	If we want to cross-compile Lighttpd or have different platforms to compile Lighttpd against, we can specify them here. Usually, we can leave these settings alone.
--enable-static --enable-shared	Makes configure build static or shared libraries to link to the Lighttpd executable. The same default is shared.
--enable-lfs	This option enables large files (above 2Gig). Set it if you host HD-movies or large genome sequence files.
--disable-ipv6	Lighttpd by default can use IPv6 in addition to the usual IPv4. Disabling it may reduce the size a little bit and quell our fears of possible bugs in the IPv6 implementation, but may leave out all users of next-gen Internet technologies in the cold.
--with-pcre	This is on by default if PCRE is available. You probably want it anyway, unless your target system is embedded.
--with-openssl	This enables SSL (usually using OpenSSL).
--with-kerberos5	This makes configure use the kerberos5 support supplied by OpenSSL.
--with-zlib --with-zlib=/usr/local/lib/	This adds libgz compression to Lighttpd (via mod_compress). If the path is omitted, configure will try to infer it.
--with-bzip --with-bzip=/opt/lib/	This adds bzip2 compression to Lighttpd (via mod_compress). See --with-zlib.
--with-fam --with-fam=/opt/fam/	This activates the use of the FAM/gamin stat cache which speeds up Lighttpd considerably on repeated requests for the same file.
--with-ldap	This allows Lighttpd to authenticate users (in mod_auth) against an LDAP directory.
--with-webdav-props --with-webdav-locks	These options enable properties and locks in WebDAV (mod_webdav).
--with-gdbm --with-memcache	These options enables the use of GDBM or memcached storage in mod_trigger_b4_dl, respectively.

Parameter (example)	Description
--with-attr	This makes Lighttpd support XFS' extended attributes to get the MIME type for a file (by mimetype.use-xattr).
--with-mysql --with-mysql=/opt/mysql/	This option adds MySQL support by mod_mysql_vhost. The optional path should contain mysql_config.
--with-lua --with-lua=/usr/src/lua	This enables the use of the Lua programming language to be embedded into lightTPD as mod_magnet.
--with-valgrind	This adds internal valgrind support. We only need this if we want to debug Lighttpd memory usage.

The make utility will use the Makefile that configure has generated to build and install Lighttpd. Configure Lighttpd to your needs, but the defaults will take care of most of them.

Building Lighttpd using CMake

Starting with 1.5.0, the Lighttpd developers tried using CMake instead of Autotools to speed up the build process. However, it was apparently removed in the development snapshots, for which Autotools are used. If we come across a version with a `CMakeLists.txt` file, we can build it using CMake.

CMake can be run with the `-i` option to start it in the wizard mode so that we are queried on all options. This is probably the easiest way of setting up Lighttpd, but depending on how many installations we have we might want to do a command-line install. In this case, `cmake -L` gives us a list of options, which we can supply via the `-D` switch, as in:

```
cmake -DWITH_OPENSSL:BOOL=OFF -DCMAKE_INSTALL_PREFIX:PATH=/home/lighty
```

Options of the type BOOL can take the values ON, OFF (or TRUE, False, Y, N, and so on). All other types are basically handled like strings. The naming of the options should be similar to the options for Automake in the preceding table.

Summary

Regardless of whether we use precompiled packages for our target operating system, or compile our own Lighttpd, the setup would not be much easier. A seasoned administrator will compile and install a basic Lighttpd in under 15 minutes (in fact even a less weathered one can do, since this is what I timed on my last attempt to install 1.4.19).

Now that we have installed our Lighttpd, let us get it up and running.

2
Configuring and Running Lighttpd

In this chapter, we will learn:

- How to configure Lighttpd
- What Selectors are
- How to use Selectors
- How to rewrite and redirect requests
- How to include variables in the configuration files

Now that you have successfully installed Lighttpd onto your system, I will show you how to configure it to serve web pages (yes, just web pages, nothing else) and expand from there. Lighttpd needs a configuration file called `lighttpd.conf`—in fact it will not run without one. To make it as simple as possible, we start with the absolute minimum:

```
server.document-root = "/var/www"
mimetype.assign = ("" => "text/html")
```

Yes, that is all. Of course you should take the path to your website as your document root. Under UNIX, `/var/www` is a probable path, while Windows users may want to put their site in a place like `C:\www\mysite`. The `mimetype.assign` statement simply says that everything is to be served as if it were an HTML page.

Put this `lighttpd.conf` into the standard directory of your system:

OS	Path to lighttpd.conf	Run script
Linux	`/etc/lighttpd/`	`/etc/init.d/lighttpd {start|stop}`
Windows	`C:\lighttpd\etc\`	`cd C:\lighttpd\bin; {start|stop}-lighttpd`
MacOS X	`/etc/lighttpd/`	`/etc/startd/lighttpd`

In Windows, all the installers that I tested put the `lighttpd.conf` file and run scripts under `C:\lighttpd` by default. However, we might want to change the Lighttpd directory to suit our system, for example, we may want to put it under "Program Files" or on another disk drive. We may alternatively put the `lighttpd.conf` file into any directory of our choice, but then the run scripts provided with Lighttpd may not work. This is not a big deal though, as we can still start Lighttpd directly from the command line. Note that under most systems, Lighttpd needs to be started from the administrator or root account so that it can listen to port 80.

Starting Lighttpd by Hand

Lighttpd can be started without the help of a startup script. The path to the Lighttpd executable depends on your system and installation. Given that it is in your path, we can start Lighttpd by using the following command:

```
lighttpd -f [full path to your config file]
```

With some distributions (especially some Windows builds), the -f option will be hardcoded, so we cannot and need not supply the configuration file path. When in doubt, refer to the documentation of the installation package.

There are also other command line options that are worth taking a look at:

Option	What Lighttpd does
`-m [directory]`	Loads modules from [directory], and proceeds to serve web pages (you will still need to give the configuration file path with `-f`).
`-p`	Pretty prints the configuration and exits.
`-t`	Tests the `lighttpd.conf` file for syntax errors and exits—this is useful before restarting Lighttpd and after changing the configuration to make sure no downtime will ensue.
`-D`	No-Daemon mode: Does not go to the background; useful for testing.
`-v`	Shows the Lighttpd version and exits—you might want to add it to the questions you post on the forum if something does not work.
`-V`	Shows the compile-time options (event/network handlers and features) and exits.
`-h`	Shows a list of configuration options and exits.

Now, run Lighttpd from the command line or with the provided startup script and point your browser of choice to http://127.0.0.1/index.html. Given that you have an index.html, you should see it in your browser. If you see it, congratulations! — you have made your first step into a bright future as a Lighttpd user.

Otherwise, we should tackle the problem methodically. First, start Lighttpd with the -t option to see if our configuration is parsed correctly; correct it if necessary. Next, see if the run script/Lighttpd startup failed. If it did, there are three possible culprits:

1. Port 80 (which is standard for HTTP) is blocked by some other application. In this case, you should see something else in your browser (given that the other application that listens on port 80 speaks HTTP).

2. Lighttpd does not have sufficient privileges to listen on port 80. Try running Lighttpd as root, or use ports higher than 1024, say, port 8080.

3. Your Lighttpd installation or package is erroneous. Try another version or visit the forum at http://forum.lighttpd.net and ask for help.

If Lighttpd starts without error, make sure that your index.html is in your document-root directory and readable by the Lighttpd instance. If that does not solve the problem, we will need some debugging to find out what has failed. To do this, extend your lighttpd.conf file to include logging and up to four debug directives:

```
server.modules += ("mod_accesslog")
server.errorlog = "/var/log/lighttpd/error.log"
                              # or wherever you want to put it
debug.log-file-not-found = "enabled"
debug.log-request-header = "enabled"
debug.log-request-handling = "enabled"
debug.log-response-header = "enabled"
```

Now, you can restart Lighttpd, browse at http://127.0.0.1/index.html, and look into your error log to see what went wrong.

Generally, setting options are done with [module].[option] = [value], where value can be a "string", a number, or a boolean (note that instead of "true" and "false" Lighttpd configuration expects "enabled" and "disabled" or a comma-separated list of values in parenthesis (like **server.modules**). You can also append values to list with [module].[option] += ([values]).

Other Core Options

There are some other core options we can set:

server.bind = "[Hostname, IP address or UNIX socket]".

This directive tells Lighttpd to bind only to specific interfaces. This may be useful if you have more than one network interface and want to bind Lighttpd only on one of them. Valid examples are:

```
server.bind = "myserver.com"   # binds to the IP found at myserver.com

server.bind = "192.168.1.81"   # binds the network interface at
                               # 192.168.1.81

server.bind = "/tmp/lighttpd.socket" # binds to a UNIX named socket
```

By default, Lighttpd binds to all network interfaces it can find. Usually, you will have only one interface. Binding to a UNIX named socket can be useful to proxy Lighttpd by some other server.

Setting server.port can change the port Lighttpd listens at. This might be useful if you cannot run Lighttpd with sufficient permissions to open ports below 1024.

```
server.port = 1234
```

The default port for unencrypted HTTP is 80, the alternate unprivileged port is 8080.

server.tag changes the so-called Server Tag that is sent with each HTTP response. It defaults to Lighttpd [version] (for example, Lighttpd 1.5.0 for version 1.5.0). If you do not want anyone to know you use Lighttpd, you can change it to anything you like.

server.name tells Lighttpd its hostname. Otherwise, the hostname or IP from the request will be used while processing the response.

server.modules is a list of modules Lighttpd will load at startup and execute on each request in the exact order they are specified. Modules are the extension mechanism Lighttpd uses to adapt to many different tasks while staying small if only a part of this power is used.

server.indexfiles may contain a list of filenames (without path) that is searched if the URI matches a directory. So if you set server.indexfiles = ("index.html"), you can enter http://127.0.0.1/ in your browser and it will still show your index.html page, given that the file exists and is readable. The first file found is served. Note that this requires the mod_indexfile module as of version 1.4.

Mime Types

To give the client a hint of what to do with a file, the HTTP protocol defines that each file should be sent with a **Mime type**. A Mime type consists of a Content type and a subtype. The Content type is one of **application, audio, example, image, message, model, multipart, text**, and **video**. Subtypes can be registered with IANA by a Web form. The **Internet Assigned Numbers Authority (IANA)** maintains a list of mime types. Most Linux or BSD systems have a local list at /etc/mime.types. The authoritative list can be found at http://www.iana.org/assignments/media-types.

> **All mime types**
>
> You can download a mime-types.py python script that uses the mime type module to create a mime type mapping suitable for inclusion in a Lighttpd configuration at http://packtpub.com/files/code/2103_Code.zip. Start the script with python mime-types.py and it writes a mime-types.conf file in the current directory.
>
> If you do not have a python interpreter, get one from http://www.python.org.

For a single web project, a fairly small map of mime types will usually suffice:

```
mimetype.assign = (
    ".html" => "text/html",
    ".txt" => "text/plain",
    ".jpg" => "image/jpeg",
    ".jpeg" => "image/jpeg",
    ".gif" => "image/gif",
    ".png" => "image/png",
    ".zip" => "application/zip",
    ".tar.gz" => "application/x-tgz",
    ".gz" => "application/x-gzip")
```

Note the last two entries; the order is of the essence here. Had we swapped them, any .tar.gz file would match .gz and would thus be served as application/x-gzip.

> **Default mime type**
>
> Using an empty extension, you can define a default mime type that will be used if no matching extension can be found, like we did in our first lighttpd.conf example.

The standard mime type for an HTML page is "text/html", but this changes if you use XHTML, which can be sent as "text/html", "text/xml" or "application/xml", the correct type being "application/xhtml+xml". Some browsers react differently on each type. Storing them with the extension ".xhtml" will make it easier to distinguish between HTML and XHTML files.

If the file system in use supports XFS-style attributes, we can set the mime type for each file with the `attr` program:

```
attr -s Content-Type -V image/jpeg foto.jpg
```

This `Content-Type` attribute can be used wherever it is present by setting

```
mimetype.use-xattr = "enable"
```

in our `lighttpd.conf` file, Lighttpd will fall back to the `mime-type.assignment` for files without `Content-Type` attribute.

Selectors

The features that make the configuration of Lighttpd very powerful, yet keep it concise, are selectors. A selector is a criterion within a curly-braced region of the configuration that only applies if the criterion is met. After the optional **else** keyword, another curly-braced region can be added that applies for the inverse of the criteria. So the basic formula for a selector is one of the following:

criteria { configuration }

or

criteria { configuration } else { configuration }

Suppose that we want to serve `.html` files from the subdirectory /xhtml of our document root as `application/xhtml+xml` and from any other directory as `text/html`:

```
mimetype.assign = (...[our list of mime types, omitting .html]...)
$HTTP["url"] =~ "^/xhtml" {
    mimetype.assign += (".html" => "application/xhtml+xml")
} else {
    mimetype.assign += (".html" => "text/html")
}
```

As we can see in the example, each criterion consists of a **value**, an **operator**, and a **pattern**. The **value** to compare is either `$SERVER["socket"]`, which matches the IP plus port (or just the port, if the IP is omitted in the pattern) or `$HTTP["x"]`, where 'x' is one of the following:

x	Description	Example value
host	The hostname of the request	`example.com`
remoteip	The IP of the client	12.34.56.78
cookie	A list of cookies	loginHash=A3DF25B
useragent	The "user-agent" header of the request	Mozilla/5.0 (Windows; U; Windows NT 5.1; en; rv:1.8.1.1) Gecko/20061204 Firefox/2.0.0.1
referer	The page that linked to here	`http://example.com/some.html`
url	The part of the URL after the hostname	`/other.html`

The example values would occur if a user with the IP address 12.34.56.78 using the english version of Mozilla Firefox 2.0.0.1 would click on a link on the page at `http://example.com/some.html` bringing him or her to `http://example.com/other.html`.

There are two pairs of operators: **==** and **!=** to check for equality and inequality respectively, of the values and the verbatim text. **=~** and **!~** match the value against a pattern using **Perl-Compatible Regular Expressions** (PCRE), and will only work if your Lighttpd is compiled with PCRE support. `=~` applies if the pattern matches and `!~` applies if the pattern does not match.

To become even more powerful, selectors can be nested, but not in any particular order. The value `$HTTP["url"]` always needs to be in the innermost selector. This is not a problem at all. Suppose you have two selectors:

```
$HTTP["url"] == "..." { $HTTP["cookie"] == "..." { ... } }
```

you can easily turn them inside out:

```
$HTTP["cookie"] == "..." { $HTTP["url"] == "..." { ... } }
```

Now, if you have an else-clause, this will not work, but remember that else clauses can be simulated by inverting the expression:

```
$HTTP["referer"] =~ "..." {
    server.document-root = "/www/referred"
} else {
    server.document-root = "/www/no_ref"
}
```

is equivalent to:

```
$HTTP["referer"] =~ "..." {
    server.document-root = "/www/referred"
}
$HTTP["referer"] !~ "..." {
    server.document-root = "/www/no_ref"
}
```

This way, we can split the else clauses apart and invert their ordering, if necessary. The following example shows a document-root based browser switch:

```
$HTTP["useragent"] =~ "MSIE" {
    server.document-root = "/www/msie"
} else $HTTP["useragent"] =~ "Opera" {
    server.document-root = "/www/opera"
} else { server.document-root = "/www/default" }
```

Alternatively, we can also set up a kind of virtual hosting by looking at the hostname and changing the document root:

```
$HTTP["host"] == "some.ourdomain.net" {
    server.document-root = "/www/some"
} else $HTTP["host"] == "other.ourdomain.net" {
    server.document-root = "/www/other"
}
```

... add as many subdomains as you like.

Excursion: Regular Expressions

 If you already know regular expressions, feel free to skip this section.

Regular Expressions, popularly known as **regexes**, **regexen**, or **regexps**, come from Noam Chomsky's formal language works. Chomsky searched for ways to formalize languages (without necessarily giving them meaning) and found that there was a class of languages that could be described by a finite automaton. This means a machine can decide if an input string is part of the language or not by only looking at each symbol once.

Due to the nature of their construction, **regular languages**, as Chomsky called them, can also be described by **regular expressions**. In fact, every regular expression constructs a regular language, and the PCRE used by Lighttpd actually builds something akin to the finite state machine to decide if the input is part of the regular language or not—that is, if the input "matches". It should be noted that the PCRE engine extends the classical regexes in a way that enables them to define some non-regular languages, thus giving them even more power.

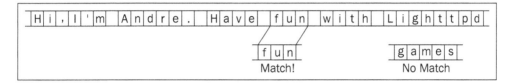

This diagram shows how regular expressions match an input text. It also goes to show that learning Lighttpd is not all fun and games (well, it's fun, but no games). The pattern needs to match only part of the input text. Most characters in the pattern match themselves. If you want to match only from the beginning, you can match the beginning itself with "^". Similarly the end is matched by a dollar-sign "$":

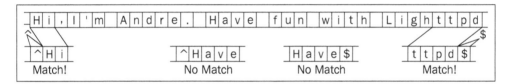

Play it Again, Sam

One of the powerful features of regexps is repetition. The pattern a+ would match a, aa, aaa, any number of as. The pattern a* matches everything a+ matches, plus the empty string. The pattern a{2,4} matches aa, aaa, and aaaa. You can of course put any value instead of 2 and 4, or even omit the second value to match the exact number of as.

Note that the *, +, and {} operators are "greedy". This means they try to match as much as possible of the first occurrence.

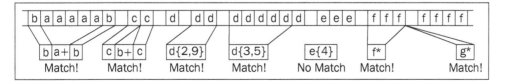

Are You There?

If you want to match something if it is there, but not lose your match if it is not, you can put a question mark "?" after it. The question mark also turns the greedy operators + and * into meek operators that match only what is absolutely needed. A period in the pattern will match one character, regardless of what it is—so, * will match everything.

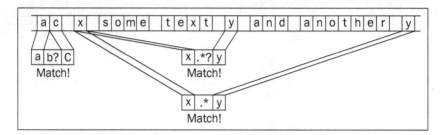

Decisions, Decisions

Sometimes we need to match either of the two values, for example www and web. The vertical bar does just that. So our pattern would read www|web. Now, if we also want to match net, we just extend our pattern with another vertical bar and get www|web|net. Note that the vertical bar binds **weaker** than the other operators, so ba*|cd+ would not match bdd. A usual case is to match a single digit, letter or other character. So, a shortcut was invented: [abc] is equal to a|b|c, [0-9] will match one digit and [a-z] will match one lowercase character. To invert the character range, use ^ at the beginning of the character group, for example [^0-9] will match one character that is not a digit. We can match, if we put it at the beginning of the range.

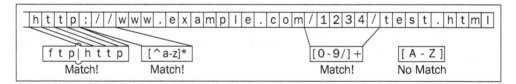

Group and Capture

Putting parenthesis around a pattern will group and capture this pattern. First, to go with the example above b(a*|c)d+ will match bdd. It will also "capture" an empty string (matched by a*) into $1. This is not very interesting for selectors but will be very useful when it comes to rewriting and redirecting. The captures are ordered by the position of the opening parenthesis.

It is also possible to create a **non-capturing group** using **?=** pattern that will match a pattern without capturing, or even a **negative group** using **?!** pattern that will only match if the pattern is not there.

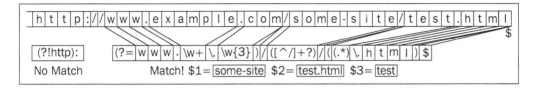

Lucky Escape

Now you might want to ask how to match against those characters that make up the operators? We can "escape" them by prefixing them with a backslash in the pattern, so they will match themselves verbatim. Also the usual C-string like escapes work as usual. The following table shows the escapes and what they mean:

Escape	Match	Escape	Match	Escape	Match	Escape	Match	Escape	Match
\\	\	\(	(	\)	)	\[	[	\]	]
\.	.	\{	{	\}	}	\?	?	|	|
*	*	\+	+	\-	-	\^	^	\$	$
\t	tabulator			\r	carriage return			\n	newline
\l	line feed			\xxy	char with hexcode xy			\e	escape

Additionally, there are some abbreviations for commonly used character classes:

Escape	Description	Escape	Description
\d	All digits	\D	All non-digits
\w	Alphanumeric + "_"	\W	Non-alphanumeric and not "_"
\s	Whitespace, newlines, tabs, and so on.	\S	Non-whitespace characters
\b	Word boundary	\B	Not on word boundary

The character classes can be mixed and matched with single characters and ranges, for example [\w\-] or [a-z\d:\.]. The word boundary matches the position between \w and \W, or vice versa:

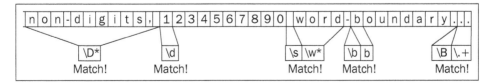

There are more tricks you can do with regular expressions—in fact there are entire books written about them. The basics presented here should be enough to understand the examples that will follow.

Testing Regular Expressions

The best way to learn regular expressions is to test them with some input. There are some programs that do this. The PCRE library comes with a "pcretest" utility that lets you enter the regular expression (note that it requires you to "quote" the regexes) and then multiple input texts.

I also use the jEdit regexp tester sometimes. To get jEdit and the regexp tester plugin, visit http://jedit.org. You can also search for "regexp test" at http://freshmeat.net to find other regular expression testing programs.

Now, we can structure our configuration with selectors and carve out regions of our server landscape using regex matching. Let us put this ability to use to rewrite and redirect requests.

Rewriting and Redirecting Requests

URLs are a part of the user interface of every website, be it a full-blown application or just a bunch of static pages. Users sometimes use URLs to navigate, say, by cutting a suffix to "move up a directory". So, we want to present them a clean structured tree. Unfortunately, reality is usually not that nice. We may have some web frameworks stitched together that require their own path names. We may want to hide from the user that she is calling a script. Whatever the reason be, mod_rewrite and mod_redirect are here to help us.

The difference between rewrite and redirect is that a rewrite happens directly in the server, while redirecting a request is done by sending a header to the user telling her where the page really is. This difference is important when deciding whether to rewrite or to redirect. If we have a kind of shortcut or a second domain name and want to direct the user to the "correct" URL, we redirect. Otherwise, we rewrite, for example to present a coherent URL tree to the user when in reality the tree is created by a parameterized CGI script or distributed across multiple directories.

Both modules share the same conventions. So we'll discuss them in one go. Before using mod_rewrite and mod_redirect, we need to tell Lighttpd to load them:

```
server.modules = ("mod_rewrite", "mod_redirect", ...)
```

Remember that the order of modules loaded is important—`mod_rewrite` and `mod_redirect` change the query URL, so they should come first. Otherwise, your request might be done with before the modules even had a chance to rewrite or redirect something.

`mod_rewrite` gives us the options `url.rewrite-once` and `url.rewrite-repeat`, `mod_redirect` provides the `url.redirect` option. It would make no sense to have `url.redirect-repeat`, as this would require keeping track of who was redirected to where. Also, if the user is redirected to himself or herself, an infinite loop would occur. All browsers I have tested guard against such infinite loops and present an error to the user. Naturally, we have to be careful with `url.rewrite-repeat`, as the rewrite happens inside the server and will stop only after a hundred iterations.

Each of these options takes a list of regex => URL pairs. The URL should be fully qualified, for example: `"http://www.example.com/mysite/"`, not `"/mysite/"`.

Remember captures from regular expressions? This is where they shine. In the URL, the expressions `$1`, `$2`, …, `$9` are expanded to the respective captures of the regex. As in:

```
url.rewrite = ("^/mysite/([^/]*)/(.*)" => "http://www.example.com/
mysite.php?x=$1&y=$2")
```

If the user browses `http://www.example.com/mysite/one/two`, the rewritten URL will be `http://www.example.com/mysite.php?x=one&y=two`.

Or it would be even better, if we put our rewrite and redirect lists into a host selector and use its captures using `%1`, `%2`, …, `%9`: for example, if we want to redirect every URL not starting with www to the same URL, but with "www." prefixed, we just add to our configuration:

```
$HTTP["host"] =~ "www\..*" {
    # we can do something for the correct URL here.
    } else $HTTP["host"] =~ "^(.*)$" {
        # we use the else here so we can capture the whole hostname.
    url.redirect = ( "^(.*)$" => "www.%1/$1" )
}
```

Now, any call to `http://example.com` will be redirected to `http://www.example.com`.

This is the beauty of Lighttpd—a set of simple, but extensible components cleverly integrated, so we do not have to learn more complicated syntax.

Of course, if you want to have a quote, dollar sign, percent sign, or backslash verbatim in your URL, you have to prefix it with a backslash to escape it. Percent signs are quite usual for URL-encoded characters (that is a percent sign followed by a hex code). For example:

```
url.rewrite = (
    "^(.*)$" => "ourdomain.net/dispatch.cgi?test=\"\%5F\"&page=$1"
)
```

You could use this method to extend the flexibility of your virtual hosting method to any possible subdomain. The trick is to rewrite the host name to be part of the document path:

```
$HTTP["host"] =~ "^(.*)\.ourdomain.net$" {
    url.rewrite = ( "^(.*)$" => "ourdomain.net/%1/$1" )
}
```

Add a directory for any subdomain you might want named exactly like the subdomain. In our example, a subdirectory named "somewhere" in the document root would be mapped to `http://somewhere.ourdomain.net`. This method has a small drawback: the error returned for undefined subdomains is a file-not-found instead of a server-not-found. A better method will be discussed in the next chapter.

Now, we can serve static pages even with virtual hosting. Our configuration file is likely to become a little bloated. Luckily, Lighttpd gives us some features to manage the complexity by including files, defining and using variables to give name values which are often used, including the output of an executable file (usually shell code) into the configuration.

Including Variables, Files, and Shell-code

Lighttpd allows us to define and use variables in its configuration files. To make it easier to distinguish between a configuration option and a variable, you have to prefix your variables with `var.` as in `var.docroot`. Later on, you can use them by simply putting them in place of whatever value you have given them. For example:

```
var.docroot = "/var/www"
server.document-root = var.docroot
```

This can be useful if you have values that appear in a lot of places. Just put them in a variable and if you need to change the value, you only need to change it in one place. We can also set and get variables of the environment. The `env` namespace is reserved for this:

```
server.document-root = env.HOME + "/htdocs" # for a user dir
server.document-root = env.LIGHTTPD_BASE + var.htmldir
    # to use an environment variable
```

You can also include files with an `include` statement:

```
include "some.conf"
```

This tells Lighttpd to parse the contents of `some.conf` as if they were in place of the include statement. You can use includes and variables together to have something like a subroutine in most programming languages. Set variables in the outer config, use them in the included config, and we have a re-usable configuration component!

For example: A virtual host has its document root in `/var/www/vhost1`, another in `/var/www/vhost2`. We could set things up for both with a small code snippet in a file we will call `vhost.conf` file:

```
$HTTP["host"] == var.vhost + ".ourdomain.net" {
    server.name = var.vhost + ".ourdomain.net"
    server.document-root = var.docroot + var.vhost
    server.follow-symlink = disabled
            # we do not trust our vhost
    accesslog.filename = var.log + var.vhost
            # log each vhost seperately
    index-file.names = ("index.html", "index.htm")
            # only HTML index files, may be different outside the vhosts
}
```

Then, our `lighttpd.conf` could include it like this:

```
#...
var.docroot = "/var/www/"
var.log = "/var/log/"

var.vhost = "vhost1"
include "vhost.conf"

var.vhost = "vhost2"
include "vhost.conf"
#...
```

Now, we have set up both virtual hosts and our `lighttpd.conf` file still looks quite tidy. It is also possible to include the output of a program into the `lighttpd.conf` file with the `include_shell` command.

This might seem like a great deal, but remember that usually you are the one starting Lighttpd, so you can also put the output of the `include_shell` command into a file and include it.

Security Alert (virtual hosting only)

If you are setting up virtual hosting and want to allow your users access to their own configuration, you need to disable or otherwise forbid this feature. Othewise, you give everyone whose configuration you include, a free root shell (given that Lighttpd is started as root, which is required for listening on port 80). You can disable this by downloading `configfile.c.patch` file from `http://www.packtpub.com/files/code/2103_Code.zip`.

Another thing variables can be useful for is distinguishing a test and production environment. You might want to run a test Lighttpd without disturbing your production Lighttpd. Variables to the rescue — put the following into `lighttpd.conf` file:

```
var.http_port = 80
var.https_port = 443
var.docroot = "/var/www/prod"
include "lighttpd_conf.conf"
```

And create a `test.conf` with:

```
var.http_port = 1080
var.https_port = 1443
var.docroot = "/var/www/test"
include "lighttpd_conf.conf"
```

Now our `lighttpd.conf` file can simply use the variables to set the ports (instead of having them plain in our file) and the document root, and then we can start a test Lighttpd that:

- Listens on different ports and will thus start while our production Lighttpd is still running.
- Does not mess with our production assets as it uses another document root.

Summary

This chapter only dealt with the configuration to serve static pages, but there are already many options to set. The relevant options can be grouped into three categories:

1. Options that tell Lighttpd where to look for a file.
2. Options that tell Lighttpd which interfaces and addresses to serve.
3. Options that tell Lighttpd how to serve content, for example,which MIME type.

We learned about includes and variables, and had a brief introduction to regular expressions that Lighttpd uses in many places.

The next chapter will discuss more ways to do virtual hosting, and how we can add dynamic content to our bag of tricks.

3
More Virtual Hosting and CGI

In this chapter, we will learn:

- How to set up virtual hosting
- How to install MySQL server and configure with Lighttpd modules
- How to configure SCGI and FastCGI with Lighttpd modules

Suppose that we want to host a lot of sites without restarting Lighttpd whenever a new site comes and goes. Given that all sites share the same configuration, we can do this using the line of **mod_*vhost** modules. To use them, we may include one of the following lines:

```
server.modules += ("mod_simple_vhost") # for simple virtual hosting

server.modules += ("mod_evhost") # for extended virtual hosting

server.modules += ("mod_mysqlvhost")
                        # for virtual hosting with a MySQL database
```

The most basic, but an already usable module is `mod_simple_vhost`. With this simple virtual hosting solution, all we have to do is to supply a server root for virtual hosting, a default host name, and a document root, like this:

```
simple-vhost.server-root = "/var/www/vhost/"
simple-vhost.default-host = "myvirtualhost.net"
simple-vhost.document-root = "htdocs"
```

`mod_simple_vhost` intercepts each request and constructs a document path out of the server root, the host name (either from the request or the default), the document root, and the file path. Given `http://some.virtualhost.net/some/file.html` as the request URL, `mod_simple_vhost` would construct the path as:

```
"/var/www/vhost"/"some.virtualhost.net"/"htdocs"/"some/file.html"
```

If the file could not be found, `mod_simple_vhost` will see if the directory `some.virtualhost.net` exists in the server root . If so, it will return a file not found error (HTTP code 404). Otherwise, it will not even answer the request, as the domain is obviously not on this server.

Extended Virtual Hosting

Too simple? Well, we can gain one level of complexity by using `mod_evhost`. The "e" stands for extended and while it does a little more than `mod_simple_vhost`, the configuration is even more minimal. In fact, there is only one option:

```
evhost.path-pattern = "/var/www/vhost/%3.%0/htdocs"
```

This example would do exactly the same as the code above, only using `mod_evhost` instead of `mod_simple_vhost`. The percent-signs with numbers are placeholders for the following values (in our example for the subdomain **some.domain. myvirtualhost.net**):

Placeholder	Value	Description
%0	"myvirtualhost.net"	The domain name including top-level-domain
%1	"net"	The top-level-domain
%2	"myvirtualhost"	The domain name without top-level-domain
%3	"domain"	The subdomain name

This implies that "%0" could also be stated as "%2.%1". We do not gain much flexibility over `mod_simple_vhost`; the most common usage is:

```
evhost.path-pattern = "/var/www/vhost/%0/%3/htdocs"
```

So, we can have a directory per-domain containing a directory for each subdomain, or if we serve only one domain, we can leave out the domain name:

```
evhost.path-pattern = "/var/www/vhost/%3/htdocs"
```

Now, we have omitted the domain name in our path. We can also use a similar pattern to create per-user homepages under `http://username.myvirtualhost.net` where every user has a home directory under `/home/username` with a subdirectory `html`:

```
evhost.path-pattern = "/home/%3/html"
```

MySQL based Virtual Hosting

To have the freedom to put our sites up anywhere we want, we can use mod_mysqlvhost. This module reads the document root for a domain from a MySQL database table and will thus need a running MySQL server. mod_mysqlvhost gives the maximum flexibility, usually at a small performance cost.

Many Web projects already use MySQL as a backend database, so the cost of running MySQL does not need to be taken into the calculation. For all other installations, the cost of running a MySQL server would probably not be worth the additional flexibility.

Installing MySQL

[If you already have a running MySQL, you can skip this section.   ]

First, we need to download MySQL. The MySQL download site, available under http://www.mysql.com/downloads/mysql/, links to mirrors that have packages for almost all systems. To pick the optimal package source, here are my recommendations:

System	Recommendation
Windows	Download "Windows (x86) ZIP/Setup.EXE" from the MySQL download site. Run the installer and create an options file in C:\Windows\my.ini (C:\WinNT\my.ini for Windows NT).
Linux (Red Hat, Ubuntu, Novell/SuSE, Debian, other popular binary distributions)	Start the package manager and install the distribution's MySQL package.
Gentoo Linux	Type emerge mysqld on the shell.
Other Linuxes	Download the static tarball from the MySQL download site.
FreeBSD	Download the static tarball from the MySQL download site.
Solaris	Download the package for your Solaris version from the MySQL download site.
Mac OS X	Download the .dmg for your CPU type from the MySQL download site.
AIX, HP-UX, Novell NetWare, QNX, SCO OpenServer	The MySQL download site has binary packages for your platform.
Others	Download the source packages from the MySQL download site. Follow the README to compile MySQL.

The options file fo Windows installations should include the following lines (given that you have installed MySQL in C:\mysql):

```
[mysqld]
basedir=C:/mysql # note the / instead of \
datadir=C:/mysql/data
```

The installers usually set up their own options file.

Bringing MySQL and mod_mysqlvhost Together

mod_mysqlvhost is as flexible as possible – you can create your database the way you want it. The only thing that is really needed is a table with at least two columns, one of which contains the domain name and the other the path. Both are usually stored as VARCHARs. A possible database setup SQL script might be:

```
GRANT SELECT ON domains.* TO lighttpd@localhost
IDENTIFIED BY '********';
CREATE DATABASE domains;
USE domains;
CREATE TABLE domains (
    domain VARCHAR(64) not null primary key,
    document_root VARCHAR(256) not null);
```

The corresponding Lighttpd configuration is:

```
mysql-vhost.db = "domains"
mysql-vhost.user = "lighttpd"
mysql-vhost.password = "********"
mysql-vhost.sock = "/var/sock/mysql.lighttpd.sock"
mysql-vhost.sql = "SELECT document_root from domains WHERE domain=?"
```

Of course, we should take a password not only consisting of asterisks. Adding, moving, and deleting domains can now be done with the following SQL:

```
# Add a domain
INSERT INTO domains
    VALUES ('subdomain.ourdomain.net', '/var/www/sub1');
# Move a domain to another directory
UPDATE domains SET document_root = '/var/www/subdomain'
    WHERE domain = 'subdomain.ourdomain.net';
# Delete a domain
DELETE FROM domains WHERE domain='subdomain.ourdomain.net';
# Change a domain name by deleting the old and adding a new entry.
```

Now we have everything in place to be completely free with our domain to document root mapping.

MySQL Administration Programs

MySQL comes with a very minimal command line client. To speak with the server more comfortably, the following programs might help:

MySQL Gui Tools come from the same folks as the MySQL database itself, so they are easily the tool of choice when it comes to working with MySQL.

phpMyAdmin from `http://phpmyadmin.net` is a CGI-based tool written in PHP. It even works with Lighttpd. To learn to install it, read chapter 9.

Java SQL Admin Tool can work with MySQL and is completely written in Java, so it "runs everywhere" according to the Sun Microsystems marketing slogan. Find it at `http://www.trash.net/~ffischer/admin/index.html`.

Under Linux, both **Gnome** and **KDE** have MySQL administration programs (Gnome MySQL client and KNoda). Lastly, go to `http://freshmeat.net` and search for "MySQL admin".

Going Dynamic

When the Internet was created, it was all a bunch of text (and later some graphics) files. Things have changed a lot since then—the majority of websites today are not primarily static sites. Either the HTML itself is created by a **Content Management System (CMS)** or the site embeds applications in the static content. To allow two-way communication between the browser and a program running on a web server, and to generate the content dynamically on the server, the **Common Gateway Interface (CGI)** was created.

CGI is very simple. The server gets a request, sets up an environment, starts the CGI process and optionally (for HTTP POST requests) pipes the request content into the CGI process' standard input. The CGI process prints the response (including headers) to its standard output, from where it is forwarded to the user by the server.

The simplicity of CGI gave it a big advantage over embedding applications in the server (as is done with Microsoft's Active Server Pages or Sun Microsystems' Java Server Pages), as one could run a CGI application over any web server supporting it, thus giving web server and web application creators a motivation to implement CGI.

With the proliferation of CGI-capable servers and applications, the downside of CGI has become apparent. CGI spawns one process per request , which taxes the operating system, memory and CPU, and leaves no chance to cache data between requests, as each CGI process starts with a clean slate.

There have been some attempts to create a successor to CGI. Two of the most successful successors are implemented as Lighttpd modules: **SCGI** and **FastCGI**.

Up to and including version 1.4.20, Lighttpd came with a module for each interface: `mod_cgi` for CGI, `mod_scgi` for SCGI, and `mod_fastcgi` for FastCGI. From version 1.5.0 onwards, these modules have ceased to exist, and `mod_proxy_core`, a shared code base for all application and proxying interfaces, has been extended by backend modules: `mod_scgi_backend` and `mod_fastcgi_backend`. Still, as at the time of this writing, 1.4.20 is in active use by many, we will start with `mod_cgi`.

CGI with mod_cgi

To enable CGI in Lighttpd, we need to include and configure the module. For example, we might want to execute all files with the `cgi` extension:

```
server.modules += ("mod_cgi")
cgi.assign = (".cgi" => "")
```

The "" in `cgi.assign` means that CGI scripts are started in their own shell. Otherwise, this entry would contain the path to the CGI interpreter/application.

We probably want to add `index.cgi` to the list of index files:

```
server.indexfiles = ("index.cgi", "index.html")
```

Alternatively, we might prefer putting all CGI programs in one directory instead of distinguishing them by extension:

```
cgi.assign = ("/cgi-bin/" => "")
                      # Patterns starting with "/" match the path.
```

If the CGI protocol is very simple, why should the configuration be any more complex?

FastCGI

The FastCGI interface was created with speed in mind, while giving a programming environment almost equal to the CGI protocol. FastCGI distinguishes between Responders and Authenticators, both of which can get a request and issue a response. However, most FastCGI applications just use the Responder part of the protocol.

A FastCGI application runs in a while-loop, with the rest of the program being written in plain CGI style. As the program runs continuously, we can store data between requests; also the setup cost is removed for all requests but the first. A typical program would look like this (in most languages):

```
<startup>
while (FCGI_Accept())
    <handle request>
<cleanup>
```

The FastCGI protocol comes with libraries for C, Perl and Java. In addition, there are FastCGI libraries in many programming languages. PHP even comes with an optional FastCGI-compatible interpreter. Visit http://www.fastcgi.org/ to find the library for your favorite language, or read Chapter 13 for real world examples.

We can configure FastCGI using mod_fastcgi with Lighttpd versions prior to 1.5.0:

```
server.modules += ("mod_fastcgi")

fastcgi.server = (
    ".cgi" => ( # suffix-match if it starts with "."
            # List of servers load-balanced by Lighttpd
            (       "host" => "localhost",      # FastCGI over TCP/IP
                    "port" => 1234 ),
            # FastCGI over UNIX domain sockets
            (       "socket" => "/var/sock/lighttpd-fcgi.sock" ),
            # FastCGI application started by Lighttpd
            (       "bin-path" => "/usr/bin/perl",
                    "docroot" => "/var/www/myperlapp" )
    ),
    "/cgi-bin" => ( # prefix-match if it starts with "/"
            ( "bin-path" => "/usr/bin/php-fcgi",
              "broken-scriptfilename" => "enable",
              "min-procs" => 1,
              "max-procs" => 4 # ... other options folllow
        )
    )
)
```

`mod_fastcgi` will load-balance the given servers. If we use the `bin-path` directive, it will even start them for us (until version 1.5.0, which comes with its own utility to do this). Let us have a detailed look at the options per server. As we see in our example, there are three ways to reach a server:

- By TCP host and port
- By UNIX domain socket, and
- By starting it from **bin-path**.

If we let Lighttpd start our FastCGI program, we also have some more options:

Option	Description
"bin-environment" => ("key1"=>"value1", ...)	Sets the environment entries in the FastCGI environment.
"bin-copy-environment" => ("key1", ...)	Copies the given environment entries to the FastCGI environment.
"min-procs" = 1 "max-procs" = 4	Starts and keeps alive at least 1 and at the most 4 instances of our FastCGI program.
"max-load-per-proc" => 3 "idle-timeout" => 120	Starts a new instance on 3 waiting requests. Kills a process if it is idle for 120 seconds.

The entry `"mode"=>"authorizer"` tells Lighttpd to treat the FastCGI program as Authorizer. We can also set `"mode" => "responder"`, but this is the default anyway. For Authorizers, the `"docroot"` entry is mandatory. For responders, it does not hurt to set `"docroot"`, especially if the FastCGI program uses it somewhere.

The `"check-local"` entry can be enabled or disabled. If it is enabled, it tells Lighttpd to look for a local file in the `"docroot"` path at the given address, and sends out a 404 error if it does not find anything. This is useful for using scripting languages as FastCGI responders.

If Lighttpd detects a server outage, it will route the requests to the remaining servers and check regularly if the broken server comes up again. We can set the duration in seconds between such checks with the `"disable-time"` entry.

For PHP, if the `"broken-scriptfilename"` entry is enabled, Lighttpd will mangle the `SCRIPT_FILENAME` FastCGI environment entry so that PHP has a correct `PATH_INFO`. The `allow-x-send-file` allows a backend to put the response in a file (perhaps a cache), set a `X-LIGHTTPD-send-file` header and have Lighttpd send out the content of this file.

`mod_fastcgi` supplies two additional global options, but we will seldom use them:

```
fastcgi.map-extensions = ("php4" => "php")
    # to handle php4 analog to php files.

fastcgi.debug = 1 # or 0 to disable debugging
```

Since the version 1.5.0, `mod_proxy`, `mod_fastcgi`, and `mod_scgi` have been pulled together to `mod_proxy_core` plus various backends. The configuration options are the same for all the modules and are explained below (*mod_proxy_core and backends*).

SCGI

The **Simple Common Gateway Interface** (**SCGI**) was created to remove the burden of starting a new process for each request while being simple to implement. Re-using the process is a big win for scripting languages, where the interpreter can stay in memory as the scripts are loaded and cached. The overall goal of SCGI is simplicity of implementation. SCGI was created as a primary interface between python web applications and web servers.

With SCGI, the headers are sent as a concatenation of pairs of zero-terminated strings, so that C programs can use them without copying. The SCGI standard does not specify how the transport between the application and the web server is implemented, as long as it carries a stream of bytes.

SCGI and FastCGI are quite similar, but SCGI gives up backward-compatibility to gain simplicity. Due to the similarities, the Lighttpd SCGI module shares the configuration options of the FastCGI module.

mod_proxy_core and backends

Since version 1.5.0, the dynamic page processing interface core functionality was consolidated into `mod_proxy_core` and only the differences between the interfaces moved into a backend for each. This reduces duplication, with some obvious benefits. Less duplicated code implies less stuff in memory, less chances for errors, more testing for the core, and optimizations apply to all interfaces.

The syntax has changed a little, for example, we no longer assign path prefixes to configurations, but use selectors to reduce the reach of the backends.

Suppose that we want to use `mod_proxy_core`, we add it to `server_modules` along with the backends we want. Then we carve out a niche for each backend and configure the backends. For example, to use SCGI for a python application and FastCGI for PHP, we write:

```
server.modules = ( ...,
    "mod_proxy_core",
    "mod_proxy_backend_fastcgi",
    "mod_proxy_backend_scgi", # see appendix B for all backends.
    ... )

$HTTP["url"] =~ ".py" { # use SCGI for python files
    proxy_core.protocol = "scgi"
    proxy-core.balancer = "carp" # tries to keep processes together
    proxy-core.backends = { # we have 3 SCGI servers to balance:
            "127.0.0.1:3456", # a local port (by IP address)
            "otherhost.mydomain.net:3456", # a port on another host
            "unix:/tmp/python.socket" # a unix socket
    }
    proxy-core.max-pool-size = 3 # for SCGI the number of backends
    # for other options, see Appendix B
}

$HTTP["url"] =~ ".php" { # use FastCGI for PHP files
    proxy_core.protocol = "fastcgi"
    proxy-core.balancer = "sqf" # tries to balance workload fairly
    proxy-core.backends = {
            "unix:/tmp/php-fastcgi.socket",
            "[::1]:4001" # on IPv6 host 1 in this network, port 4001
    }
    proxy-core.max-keep-alive-requests = 8
            # analog to server.max-keep-alive-requests, see chapter 9
    proxy-core.allow-x-sendfile = "enable" # see chapter 9
}
```

The use of selectors gives us greater freedom on when to use which backend, and the uniform syntax makes it easy to learn and use.

Summary

In this chapter, we have learned how to set up virtual hosting—from totally simple with `mod_simple_vhost` to absolutely flexible with `mod_mysql_vhost`. As in most circumstances we can control where our Web projects are, the simplest solution will usually suffice. Lastly, we can use simple selectors, which give us a lot more control on what modules we want to allow for which site, but need a reload of the configuration for every domain change.

Then, we had a brief look at the web application interfaces that Lighttpd offers and discussed how they can be configured in different Lighttpd versions. Chapter 11 will present detailed usage examples for common applications and programming languages.

4
Downloads and Streams

A huge section of the Internet is reserved for downloadable and streamable content. Music, images, movies, programs, and things we have not thought about yet are made available (maybe for a small fee or through their advertisements) as a direct download. Music and movies (the latter often in flash video or short `flv` format) can also be streamed. Sites like YouTube, using Lighttpd to serve video files, show that Lighttpd has got what it takes to do this job.

Large files present a special scenario to our Lighttpd: we will have less, but bigger requests. Some users will use download managers that create a number of HTTP range requests in parallel to optimize against bandwidth restrictions some providers operate with. We may or may not want to allow that, especially if our throughput is high. In that case each additional connection from one user will take resources away from all the others. On the other hand, we may want to allow range requests, to let our customers resume broken downloads.

If we want to serve large files, we need to set the write timeouts higher than usual — to compensate for the longer time the transfer will need. We may also want to use the `writev` network backend or one of the `aio` backends in the new version.

Keep large content static

This message is probably obvious. But do not try serving large files dynamically. It just hogs our Lighttpd plus a backend job squeezes a large amount of bytes through two sockets or pipes.

Core Settings

Using this scenario as a starting point, we will enumerate the knobs to be turned. Here are some configuration settings that will make our Lighttpd serve large files faster and more reliably than the defaults. First, we make sure range requests are enabled using the following command:

```
# if we have disabled range requests for some reason:
server.range-requests = "enable"
```

We want to use the optimal network backend for sending out content. If in doubt, take a file of the size we want to serve or create (for example, we can use dd to create a 1GB file):

$ dd if=/dev/zero of=our_file bs=1024 count=10480576

Now, put this file into our document root and run an http_load test (refer to Chapter 9 for further details) with each network backend that we get to run. Then, pick the fastest network backend. Probably it is one of the following, depending on your system. Take your pick and be sure to test on our system; when in doubt, test all of them:

```
server.backend = "writev"                # optimal for 1.4 versions
server.backend = "posix-aio"             # the fastest for large files
server.backend = "gthread-aio"           # using threads to multiplex
server.backend = "linux-aio-sendfile"    # optimized for linux
```

 Each backend uses a different strategy to optimize throughput. On POSIX-compatible systems, posix-aio is, at least for the time being, the fastest backend for large files.

In the next step, ramp up the idle write timeouts:

```
server.max-write-idle = 720              # double to 12 minutes.
```

This allows clients to keep a connection-on-hold a little longer, which they might do for any old reason (for example, their network might be down for a second), without killing their download. On the other hand, we might want to reduce the maximum keep-alive requests to free up connections sooner (because we will not have as many requests, but the ones we have will last longer):

```
server.max-keepalive-requests = 8        # half the requests
  # if we have a different setting than the default, set
server.max-keepalive-idle = 5            # seconds
```

This should be all it needs to make our Lighttpd large-file friendly. Note that some of the settings may be pessimizations in other scenarios, for example, say some small requests. Therefore, we might want to limit the impact of these options to where we need them.

> **Multiple configurations**
>
> All the above settings have a connection scope, which is that we can put them into selectors. This means that we can have some areas optimized for large content, and other areas optimized for lots of small requests, for example, AJAX applications.

Traffic Shaping

We may either want to set up an anonymous download zone, where download speeds are throttled, and a high-speed zone for our paying customers, or we may just keep our server within a monthly budget. To achieve these goals, we can use the following settings:

```
server.kbytes-per-second = 1024        # for all connections
connection.kbytes-per-second = 32      # per connection
```

And disable the settings within a selector for the paying customers:

```
server.kbytes-per-second = 0           # disabled traffic shaping
connection.kbytes-per-second = 0
```

Note that since Lighttpd version 1.5.0, mod_evasive has gained the functionality to let a response header with the name of X-LIGHTTPD-KBytes-per-second be used as value for the connection speed setting. To enable this, we add the following to our configuration:

```
speed.just-copy-header = "enable"
```

However, this solution will turn very complex for most cases. If a user complains of slow downloads, is Lighttpd the problem, or was the X-LIGHTTPD-KBytes-per-second header wrong? Unless we want to calculate the speed for every user, we are better off with a direct setting.

Some users will use download managers that try to open a multitude of connections to bypass throughput limits. To keep those users at bay, we need a way of limit the number of connections per user. As of Lighttpd version 1.4.9, we can use mod_evasive to do this:

```
server.modules = (..., "mod_evasive", ...)
evasive.max-conns-per-ip = 2           # limit connections per IP
```

This will still give maximum throughput of 64 kilobytes per second per user, up to 16 simultaneous users. To keep our paying users at the maximum download speed, we can limit the reach of this configuration through selectors, as the tip from above also applies here.

Still, there is a problem with this approach because some users trying to download simultaneously may sit behind a proxy as their IP address is same. The mod_extforward module handles this by letting us add a list of trusted proxies, so that the X-forwarded for header value will be used as a client IP:

```
# the order matters, otherwise mod_accesslog and mod_evasive
# will get the proxy IP instead of the client IP
server.modules  = (
  ...
 "mod_accesslog",
 "mod_evasive",
  "mod_extforward",
  ...
)
# trust proxy at 1.2.3.4
extforward.forwarder = (
    "1.2.3.4" => "trust",
)
```

We could also tell mod_extforward to trust all proxies with an extforward. forwarder entry of "all" => "trust". However, the documentation warns us that this is a bad idea, and here is why: a bad user could set up her own proxy that gives each request a new X-forwarded for IP address to fool our Lighttpd into thinking it is serving different users, annulling the effect of mod_evasive. Worse, if we use the client IP for session handling, they could hijack other legitimate users' sessions.

In a normal setting, it should suffice to start with a list of well-known proxies (search the Internet for "proxy server" or even start with an empty list) and add proxies to the list when users complain.

Showing Directory Contents

If we have a download directory and want to easily serve an up-to-date listing of its contents, mod_dirlisting can do the job. It is configurable with the header and footer, custom CSS, and exclude filters (which should usually match our mod_access settings, to hide inaccessible files from the listing).

> **mod_dirlisting versus Large Directories**
>
> Since Lighttpd is single-threaded, while the directory listing gets created, no other work is done by Lighttpd, as with all modules. Therefore, use mod_dirlisting only for small download directories—less than 100 entries should be a good rule of thumb. Otherwise, use a script through one of the CGI backends, which can run independently from Lighttpd.

Let us get straight to an example configuration of mod_dirlisting. In this example, we want to activate mod_dirlisting for the download directory, show a hidden HEADER.txt file (if there is one in the directory) before the listing, show "dotfiles" (starting with a ".") in the listing, but hide files ending with "~" or ".old", and use a custom CSS and footer:

```
server.modules += ("mod_dirlisting") # add mod_dirlisting to modules

$HTTP["url"] =~ "(^|/)/download/" {
  dir-listing.activate = "enable" # enable dirlisting
  dir-listing.hide-dotfiles = "disable"
  # show files starting with "."
  dir-listing.exclude = ("~$", "\.old$")
  # hide files ending with "~" or ".old"

  dir-listing.external-css = "/css/dir.css" # use custom CSS

  dir-listing.show-header = "enable"
  # show the contents of the HEADER.txt file before the dirlisting
  dir-listing.hide-header-file = "enable"
  # hide the HEADER.txt file from the dirlisting

  dir-listing.set-footer = "Thanks for trusting
                        <a \href=\"http://ourdomain.com\">us</a>!"
  # show a custom footer (the HTML code is inserted directly)

  dir-listing.encoding = "utf-8"
  # oh, and show the whole thing encoded in UTF-8.
}
```

This shows a fair amount of configuration options for `mod_dirlisting`. Here is the complete table of options. The first few options enable the listing and select the files that are shown or hidden, while the remaining options change the display of the listing:

Option name	Default / useful value	Description
dir-listing.activate server.dir-listing	"disable"	Each option enables showing a listing if a directory is requested.
dir-listing.hide-dotfiles	"enable"	Hides files starting with a dot.
dir-listing.exclude	("^~", ".old$")	A list of regular expressions (refer to Chapter 2). Filenames that match will be hidden from the listing.
dir-listing.hide-header-file	"disable"	Hides the "HEADER.txt" file from the listing.
dir-listing.hide-readme-file	"disable"	Hides the "README.txt" file from the listing.
dir-listing.show-header	"disable"	Shows the contents of the "HEADER.txt" above the listing.
dir-listing.show-readme	"disable"	Shows the contents of the "README.txt" below the listing, but above the footer.
dir-listing.set-footer	server.tag "Lighttpd 1.4.19"	HTML code to be written below the listing, defaults to server.tag, if any; else to the "Lighttpd " + version.
dir-listing.encoding	"iso-8859-1"	Selects the encoding of the generated HTML code.
dir-listing.external-css	"/css/dir.css"	Uses a custom CSS.

These options allow us to customize almost everything. The listing will show subdirectories first, then the files. The files will be shown with the name (which is linked to the file itself), last modification time, size, and MIME type.

```
Index of /

Name                Last Modified          Size   Type
Parent Directory/                           -      Directory
here.pdf            2008-Sep-16 21:32:38    13.6M  application/pdf
is.html             2008-Sep-16 21:33:39    36.5K  text/html
just.avi            2008-Sep-16 21:31:45    72.0M  video/x-msvideo
this_example.png    2008-Sep-16 21:32:58    402.4K image/png

Thanks for trusting us!
```

The generated HTML code contains a number of style classes to customize the display in the external CSS. The CSS style included by default, if no external CSS is set, should provide a good starting point:

```
a, a:active {text-decoration: none; color: blue;}
a:visited {color: #48468F;}
a:hover, a:focus {text-decoration: underline; color: red;}
body {background-color: #F5F5F5;}
h2 {margin-bottom: 12px;}
table {margin-left: 12px;}
th, td { font: 90% monospace; text-align: left;}
th { font-weight: bold; padding-right: 14px; padding-bottom: 3px;}
td {padding-right: 14px;}
td.s, th.s {text-align: right;}
div.list { background-color: white; border-top: 1px solid #646464;
           border-bottom: 1px solid #646464; padding-top: 10px;
           padding-bottom:14px;}
div.foot { font: 90% monospace; color: #787878; padding-top: 4px;}
```

Here is a complete list of CSS classes and their corresponding HTML elements:

HTML element, CSS class	Description
pre.header	A preformatted text area to show the contents of the HEADER.txt file, if activated
h2	The heading "Index of " + path is an h2 element
div.list	A div containing the listing
table	The table containing the entries of the dir-listing
thead, tr th	The heading for the table
tbody, tr	The content of the table
td.n	The cells of the name column
td.m	The cells of the time of the last modification column
td.s	The cells of the size column
td.t	The cells of the MIME type column

Armed with this knowledge, we can make our listing beautiful, or at least colorful. But how do we protect our download area from deep linking, and separate our paying customers from the anonymous freeloaders? Lighttpd offers not one, but two modules to secure our valuable download.

Securing Downloads

The two modules that Lighttpd offers require that a user must first get permissions to download, and have to do so within a specified window of time after which the permission times out. The difference is in the way of getting permission: `mod_trigger_b4_dl` just defines a trigger URL that a user must visit before the download is permitted, while `mod_secdownload` validates against a token to be created by a backend application (for example, our login for paying customers). Therefore, we can use `mod_trigger_b4_dl` to fight deep linking and `mod_secdownload` to differentiate between user groups.

First, let us start with `mod_trigger_b4_dl`. Let us presume that we want everyone to view (well, we cannot really control that, but at least download) a certain advertisement, for example, an image at the path `/ads/342hgf.gif`, before they can access any of our high-quality content within the next 10 seconds. We can get this to work with the following configuration:

```
server.modules += ("mod_trigger_b4_dl")
trigger-before-download.gdbm-filename = "/web/internal/ad_trigger.db"
trigger-before-download.trigger-url = "^/ads/342hgf.gif"
trigger-before-download.download-url = "^/download/"
trigger-before-download.deny-url = "/sorry.html"
trigger-before-download.trigger-timeout = 10
```

`mod_trigger_b4_dl` needs a place to store the IP addresses of the users who are downloading. We have a choice between using a `memcache` host or a GDBM database. In this case, we use the GDBM support, which has to be compiled (refer to Chapter 1), and then we set the `gdbm-filename` to a database file.

Note that GDBM is available on most systems by default; if our system lacks it, we can get it from `http://www.gnu.org/software/gdbm/`. If we do not have a GDBM database file at the path where `trigger-before-download.gdbm-filename` points to, `mod_trigger_b4_dl` will create one for us automatically.

If we have a `memcache` host and `libmemcache` support compiled into our Lighttpd (again, refer to Chapter 1), we can alternatively use it to store the IP addresses. In this case, replace the line:

```
trigger-before-download.gdbm-filename = "/web/internal/ad_trigger.db"
```

With:

```
trigger-before-download.memcache-hosts =
                ("memcache.ourdomain.net:2345") # a list of hosts
trigger-before-download.memcache-namespace = "ad-trigger"
```

Then, put the memcache hosts we want to use into the list. Both the methods work. The performance impact of one method over another is negligible, so use memcache if we already have a memcache host up and running (and possibly used for other things, too); otherwise use GDBM.

In either case, the IP addresses are stored along with a timestamp, and each time the download URL is invoked, all stored timestamps are checked. Timestamps older than the trigger-timeout are discarded from the database or memcache. If the IP address is found, and the entry has not timed out, the handling of the download URL is resumed; else a temporary redirect to the deny-url gets sent out.

The following diagram shows the process:

(1) The user connects to our server and surfs to a mod_trigger_b4_dl-enabled site. If the user (2) visits the trigger URL, (3) the hit is recorded in the database and he or she can (4) access the download. Otherwise, he or she is (5) redirected to the deny URL.

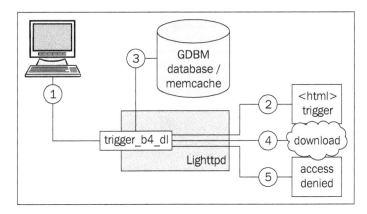

In our example, a client trying to download a file from the download directory without fetching the ads/342hgf.gif image would be redirected to http://ourdomain.com/sorry.html.

Possible Accessibility Issue

Requiring the client to download a graphic may lock out text-only browsers, which are often used by the visually impaired, for little benefit. Using an index.html as the trigger file may be a better choice unless the downloads we seek to protect are themselves of visual nature, for example, movies or images.

Anyway, here is a table of all the configuration options of `mod_trigger_b4_dl`:

Option name	Default / Example	Description
.trigger-url	"/index.html"	The URL that permits the download for the client's IP until `trigger-timeout`
.download-url	"^/download/"	A regular expression that matches the download to secure from deep linking
.deny-url	"/deny.html"	The URL that any client that has not loaded `trigger-url` within the timeout gets redirected to when trying to access the download
.trigger-timeout	10	the permission to access the secured content is valid in number of seconds
.gdbm-filename	"/path/to/trigger.db"	The path to a GDBM database file to store the actual permissions
.memcache-hosts	("127.0.0.1:2345")	A list of `memcache` hosts to store the actual permissions
.memcache-namespace	"trigger"	A unique `memcache` namespace
.debug	"disable"	Enable to show debugging info in the error log

Now that we can fight deep linking, we will put `mod_secdownload` to use by allowing access to a restricted download area to our paying customers.

The `mod_secdownload` module was created to solve a dilemma. Static downloads can only be secured from anonymous access by HTTP authentication, which is cumbersome and inflexible. On the other hand, if we use a web application to authorize the download, we also need to push all those bytes through our web application, keeping up two connections (one to the client and one to the backend) and processing data twice, which is a bad way of spending our system resources.

Now with the `mod_secdownload` module, we can have our cake and eat it, too. This is done by splitting the tasks of authentication and authorization—authentication is still done in our web application, which then computes a token that is included in the URL for the download. `mod_secdownload` will then check the token and let Lighttpd serve the download directly if it is valid. Since the download is served by Lighttpd, we get the speed of static downloads and the authentication of our web application.

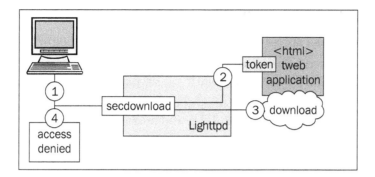

(1) The user requests the download. (2) `mod_secdownload` redirects the request to the web application page, which returns an authentication link (for example, as rewrite). `mod_secdownload` then validates the link. If the link is valid, (3) `mod_secdownload` rewrites the download link to the download directory, from which Lighttpd serves the download as a static file. If the link is invalid, (4) access is denied.

The whole process is quite simple, apart from the calculation of the token, which is also made easy by the fact that the computation uses some well-known algorithms.

The `mod_secdownload` module documentation (which can be read online at `http://trac.lighttpd.net/trac/wiki/Docs%3AModSecDownload`) contains three code listings in PHP, Ruby, and Python. Here is the corresponding Lua magnet implementation using the MD5 library of the Kepler Project (refer to Chapter 12 for further information):

```
require("md5") # for hash function
prefix = "/download/" # change this to match our configuration
secret = "change this" # as we really should

function gen_sec_link(relpath)
   if not relpath:match("^/") then relpath = "/" .. relpath end
   local time = string.format("%x", os.time())
   local token = md5.sumhexa(secret .. relpath .. hextime)
   return string.format("%s%s/%s%s", prefix, token, time, relpath)
end
```

In our further code, we can just generate a link to `"WeLoveLighttpd.avi"` using the `gen_sec_link` function like this:

```
link = gen_sec_link("WeLoveLighttpd.avi")
```

Which will generate a link to some URL that should look like the following:

```
/download/4b75945527344cf16fa08cc62ef83f51/48cec3fe/WeLoveLighttpd.avi
```

On the Lighttpd side, we will configure `mod_secdownload` to:

- Disallow direct access to `/download/` and everything below this directory

- Allow access to `"/download/"` + `token` + `timestamp` + `relpath`, rewriting the URL on the fly to `"/download/"` + `relpath`

- Send a `403 (Forbidden)` header on wrong tokens, a `408 (Request Timeout)` for Lighttpd versions prior to 1.5.0, and a `410 (Gone)` as of this version on requests after their timeout.

This is done by the following settings:

```
server.modules = (..., "mod_secdownload", ...)

secdownload.secret = "change this"              # we still should
secdownload.document-root = "/web/ourserver/"
secdownload.uri-prefix = "/download/"
secdownload.timeout = 120
```

By the way, if we do not want to make our links very complicated, we may also set a cookie in the application and match `mod_secdownload` with `mod_rewrite` to get the cookie contents into our URL. For this, we need to make sure that `mod_rewrite` gets called before `mod_secdownload` and uses a special rewrite rule:

```
server.modules = (..., "mod_rewrite", ..., "mod_secdownload", ...)

# set a global document root
server.document-root = "/web/ourserver"

# insert a set download cookie into the URL
$HTTP["cookie"] =~ "download/([0-9a-f]){32}/([0-9a-f]){8}" {
  url.rewrite = ("/download/(.*)$" => "/download/%1/%2/$1")
}

# configure secdownload
secdownload.secret = "change this, too"         # well...
secdownload.document-root = server.document-root
secdownload.uri-prefix = "/download/"
secdownload.timeout = 120
```

Now, the user will see only the `http://ourserver.com/download/file.pdf` URL, while `mod_secdownload` will get the full URL. Also, we can make the cookie expire after 120 seconds; so the timeout of the cookie and `mod_secdownload` are synchronized.

We now have everything we need to authorize downloads and streams, which we will look at in the following section.

Streaming Content

There are different solutions for streaming flash videos. Dedicated streaming servers, an apache module, and different CGI-backend-based solutions have sprung up. Of course, Lighttpd plays this game, too, with `mod_flv_streaming`. The configuration is as simple as it gets:

```
# add mod_flv_streaming to our module list
server.modules = (..., "mod_flv_streaming", ...)

# set a list of extensions to stream
flv-streaming.extensions = ( ".flv" )
```

That's it. Now we need a player that works with our streaming protocol. Fabian Topfsted has written such a player, and has made it available for noncommercial purposes at `http://www.topfstedt.de/weblog/?page_id=208`. The site has everything we need to know about setting up and embedding the player into our pages.

Apart from that, we need to be sure that our videos have the metadata (byte position of the first frame in the file, kilobytes per second, and so on) embedded in the beginning. For flash video, which keeps a constant bitrate, the playing position can then be set freely. H.264 video, which has variable bitrates, can only be played from start to end.

There are some tools to convert videos to the `flv` format and change the metadata:

- MPlayer/MEncoder at `www.mplayerhq.hu` is a fairly minimal player/encoder combo that is quite fast and plays or encodes almost everything with a minimal user interface and lots of command line options.

- **yamdi** (short for **"Yet Another MetaData Injector for FLV"**) is a command line tool to inject metadata to FLV files. It is pretty fast, because it reads only what it needs. Download it from `http://yamdi.sourceforge.net`.

- FLVTool2, located at `http://inlet-media.de/flvtool2` is another utility for FLV metadata. FLVTool2 is written in Ruby, and is thus platform-agnostic. It may not be the fastest tool, but it does the job.

- FLVMDI is a Windows-based tool with a GUI that sets and shows FLV metadata. The homepage at `http://www.buraks.com/flvmdi` has the documentation and the downloads.

This is it. We can now go and build our own YouTube. Or whatever site we may want to enhance with FLV streams.

Putting it All Together

As we have seen on the last pages, Lighttpd has a lot to offer for setting up a download or streaming server. But we might be puzzled about how they relate to each other, and how we can use them together for optimal benefit. Therefore, here is a huge example configuration that has it all:

```
# use all modules we need
server.modules = (...,
  "mod_rewrite", "mod_trigger_b4_dl", "mod_flv_streaming",
  "mod_evasive", "mod_extforward", "mod_secdownload", "mod_alias",
  "mod_accesslog", ...)

server.document-root = "/web/public"

# use the rewrite trick
$HTTP["cookie"] =~ "download/([0-9a-f]){32}/([0-9a-f]){8}" {
  url.rewrite = ("/download/(.*)$" => "/download/%1/%2/$1")
} else {
  # rewrite to avert mod_secdownload
  url.rewrite = ("^/download/" => "/freeload/")
}

# configure mod_secdownload
secdownload.secret = "foo bar qux!!!1one!eleven"
secdownload.document-root = server.document-root
secdownload.uri-prefix = "/download/"
secdownload.timeout = 120

# configure mod_dirlisting
dir-listing.exclude = ("~$", "\.old$")
dir-listing.show-header = "enable"
dir-listing.hide-header-file = "enable"
dir-listing.external-css = "/css/dir.css"
# or use a dir listing generator
# (see chapter 3 for PHP configuration)
# server.index_files = ("index.html", "/dirlisting.php")

$HTTP["url"] =~ "^/download/([0-9a-f]){32}/([0-9a-f]){8}/" {
  # paying customers, full speed
  server.backend = "posix-aio"
  server.kbytes-per-second = 0
  connection.kbytes-per-second = 0
```

```
  # make it easy on the paying customer
  server.max-write-idle = 720

  # they pay, we trust
  extforward.forwarder = ("all" => "trust")

  dir-listing.activate = "enable"
  dir-listing.set-footer = "Thanks for trusting <a\
href=\"http://ourdomain.com\">ourdomain.com</a>!"

  # finally, allow streaming
  flv-streaming.extensions = ( ".flv" )

} else $HTTP["url"] =~ "^/freeload" {
  # also downloads, so use the best backend
  server.backend = "posix-aio"

  # re-redirect internally to circumvent mod_secdownload. We could
  # also use a different directory with symbolic links
  alias.url = ("/freeload" => "/download")

  # anonymous freeloaders, support by ads
  trigger-before-download.gdbm-filename =  "/web/internal/ad_trigger.
db"
  trigger-before-download.trigger-url = "^/ads/"
  trigger-before-download.download-url = "^/download/"
  trigger-before-download.deny-url = "/no-ads-no-downloads.html"
  trigger-before-download.trigger-timeout = 5

  dir-listing.activate = "enable"
  dir-listing.set-footer = "Why not <a\
href=\"http://ourdomain.com/sign.html\">sign up</a>?"

  # also traffic-shape, make it sloooow
  server.kbytes-per-second = 1024
  connection.kbytes-per-second = 32
  evasive.max-conns-per-ip = 2

  # and throttle keepalives to close sessions earlier
  server.max-keepalive-requests = 8
  server.max-keepalive-idle = 5

  # allow streaming anyway
  flv-streaming.extensions = ( ".flv" )
}
```

With this configuration, our Lighttpd is a true download server. Note that most of this configuration has little or no side effects. So we can also use our Lighttpd for other purposes in parallel. By the way, if you want to use the above configuration, download the `downloadserver.conf` file from `http://www.packtpub.com/files/code/2103_Code.zip`.

Summary

Lighttpd offers superb download performance as well as some unique features to make it one of the best HTTP servers for download archives. Using `mod_flv_streaming`, we can also stream flash movies directly; no additional server required.

We can shape traffic, evade lechers and deep link, allow proxy servers, and use our web application to authorize customers using `mod_evasive`, `mod_trigger_b4_dl`, `mod_extforward`, and `mod_secdownload`. All of them give us terrific functionality for a very small performance cost.

5
Big Brother Lighttpd

Considering all the recent debate over privacy and data security, this chapter on how to spy on our users might seem a little off-beat. Still, there are valid reasons for wanting to know more about our users. And of course, Lighttpd can help us in our quest for this knowledge. But to stay with the zeitgeist, first a few lines about data protection.

Privacy

The early definition of privacy was "the right to be let alone". But since the late nineties of the nineteenth century, a lot has changed. As we create a bigger and bigger "data shadow" just by living normally, it becomes more about "the right to claim ownership of data about oneself". And data is a very malleable concept these days.

In short, we should take the means to try and keep the data about the site visitors to the minimum, to ensure a working site. We need not even store personal data; in most countries it is quite possible to match a person to an IP-address. Moreover, we should not gather more information about our visitors than necessary to process their requests.

But why, I hear some of you asking, shouldn't we gather the information? There is nobody other than us to read it anyway. In general, this may be true, but where I live, numerous illegal lists with personal data have made it into the news, while companies which got broken into because of shoddy security had to pay out high sums as compensation. Hackers are increasingly targeting sites to get access to the customer database. So giving them nothing for their work is a winning proposition.

With that out of the way, let us take a look at how to learn more about our users to enhance their experience.

O Browser, Where Art Thou?

Early methods to find out where users are resident involved a reverse DNS lookup and use of the Top-Level-Domain (which in many but not all cases were country domains) to find the country. These methods worked sometimes. They, however, broke down when a visitor came from a `.com`, `.org`, `.gov`, `.edu`, `.info` domain or any other non-country domain. Plus, some providers now use a `.tv` domain just for the heck of it, placing all their customers in Tuvalu on our radar.

With `mod_geoip`, we can attach a Geo-IP-database to Lighttpd to find out where our visitors are based directly from their IP address. This works much better and does not need a DNS lookup (which is quite time-consuming, involving yet another network call, with the likelihood of failure at times).

`mod_geoip` is not part of the standard distribution of Lighttpd. We have to download and install it manually. If we use Lighttpd version 1.5, we have to get the file `http://trac.lighttpd.net/trac/attachment/wiki/Docs/ModGeoip/mod_geoip.4.c`; for earlier versions, get `http://trac.lighttpd.net/trac/attachment/wiki/Docs/ModGeoip/mod_geoip.5.c`. Put this file in the `src` directory of the unpacked Lighttpd source.

Also, we need the GeoIP C Api and a database. We can get both these from the GeoIP database website. Regarding the database, we have to decide between a 570 kilobyte-sized database containing only IP and country information, and a 17.2 megabyte database that includes city information (both gzipped). Here is a list of links:

URL	What
`http://www.maxmind.com/download/geoip/database/GeoIP.dat.gz`	GeoIP Database, country information only
`http://www.maxmind.com/download/geoip/database/GeoLiteCity.dat.gz`	GeoIP Database, with city information
`http://www.maxmind.com/download/geoip/api/c/GeoIP.tar.gz`	The latest version of the C API

The C API needs to be compiled and installed, too. Unzip the `GeoIP.tar.gz` file and perform the usual installation steps (the following command line example assumes GeoIP version 1.4.5):

```
$ tar xzf GeoIP.tar.gz
$ cd GeoIP-1.4.5
$ ./configure && make && make install
checking for a BSD-compatible install... /usr/bin/install -c
checking whether build environment is sane... yes
checking whether make sets $(MAKE)... yes
... (more messages from configure and make omitted for brevity) ...
```

We may also want to put the database into some directory, which will later be included in our Lighttpd configuration, for example, /opt/geoip/. Do not forget to gunzip the database file.

As the installation routine for mod_geoip is not included in the standard Lighttpd source distribution, we need to add it to the automake definitions. This is done by adding the following to src/Makefile.am at the end of the file:

```
lib_LTLIBRARIES += mod_geoip.la
mod_geoip_la_SOURCES = mod_geoip.c
mod_geoip_la_LDFLAGS = -module -E -avoid-version -no-undefined
mod_geoip_la_LIBADD = $(common_libadd) -lGeoIP
```

Then we need to go into the Lighttpd source directory and rebuild the configure script. Finally, we can configure, compile, and install our Lighttpd. For the configure script, we need to enable the maintainer mode, so automake will find mod_geoip.

```
$ aclocal && automake -a && autoconf
$ ./configure -enable-maintainer-mode
checking build system type... i686-pc-linux-gnu
checking host system type... i686-pc-linux-gnu
checking target system type... i686-pc-linux-gnu
checking for a BSD-compatible install... /usr/bin/install -c
checking whether build environment is sane... yes
... (more messages from configure omitted for brevity) ...
$ make && make install
cd . && /bin/sh /home/andre/lighttpd-1.4.19/missing --run autoheader
rm -f stamp-h1
touch config.h.in
cd . && /bin/sh ./config.status config.h
config.status: creating config.h
make  all-recursive
... (a lot of messages from make omitted for brevity) ...
```

Now that we have installed mod_geoip, we can use it to resolve IP addresses into location information, which is then placed in the environment. Add mod_geoip to our server.modules and set the path to our database (mod_geoip will figure out autonomously which type of database we feed it):

```
server.modules += ("mod_geoip")
geoip.db-filename = "/opt/geoip/GeoLiteCity.dat"
```

This should be enough to get some new request headers in our environment. The whole configuration of mod_geoip is as follows:

Option	Default / Example	Description
geoip.db-filename	"/opt/geoip/GeoIP.dat"	The path to our GeoIP database file.
geoip.memory-cache	"disable"	Enable to let mod_geoip cache the database in memory for fast access

Configure mod_geoip and restart Lighttpd. The following request parameters will be set based on the client IP address:

Header Key	Example	Description / Example
GEOIP_COUNTRY_CODE	GB	ISO 3166 country code (alpha-2)
GEOIP_COUNTRY_CODE3	GBR	ISO 3166 country code (alpha-3)
GEOIP_COUNTRY_NAME	United Kingdom	The complete country name
The following request parameters are set only if we use a city database:		
GEOIP_CITY_NAME	Alfreton	The city where the server resides
GEOIP_CITY_POSTAL_CODE	DE55	Postal code of the city
GEOIP_CITY_LATITUDE	53.1	Latitude of the location
GEOIP_CITY_LONG_LATITUDE	-1.3833	Longitude of the location
GEOIP_CITY_DMA_CODE		DMA code (where applicable)
GEOIP_CITY_AREA_CODE		Area code (where applicable)

For more information on the ISO 3166 country codes, see the discussion at http://en.wikipedia.org/wiki/ISO_3166-1.

As of Lighttpd version 1.5, the configuration is in the global scope, otherwise, Lighttpd may hang. Also the request parameters registered by mod_geoip cannot be used in configuration selectors. However, we can use a mod_magnet script or a CGI backend program to make use of the information. For example, here is a mod_magnet script that redirects based on country code:

```lua
-- redir-country.lua mod_magnet script
-- redirect-by-country, default to "us"
local countryCode = string.lower(
  lighty.env("GEOIP_COUNTRY_CODE") or "us")
lighty.header["Location"] = string.gsub(
  lighty.env["request.uri"] or "",
  "^(www%.)?", countryCode .. ".")
return 302
```

Note that this magnet script should only attract connections to ourdomain.com or www.ourdomain.com. This can be ensured by placing the attractor in a selector on host:

```
server.modules = (..., "mod_magnet", ...) # add mod_magnet

# match only ourdomain.com and www.ourdomain.com
$HTTP["host"] =~ "^(www\.)?ourdomain.com" {
  magnet.attract-raw-url-to = "/www/magnetscripts/redir-country.lua"
} else $HTTP["host"] =~ "(\w\w)\.ourdomain.com" {
  url.rewrite = ("^(.*)$" => "/%1/$1")
}
```

The else part is mapping the country-code domains to subdirectories of the document root. Now all we have to do is create the directories for each country code containing everything we want. Alternatively, we could use a web application to match the country codes to languages.

Access Logging

We can configure logging to include more or less information. By default, Lighttpd uses the **Common Log Format** (**CLF**) as used by most available HTTP servers with varying extensions. However, the access logging is completely configurable.

If we do not care about logging, or, we are really strapped for disk space (for example, on embedded systems) we can turn it off entirely by removing mod_accesslog from our server.modules (on embedded systems we would go one step further and remove mod_accesslog entirely). Otherwise, we can configure logging to strike a balance between space and use privacy requirements on one hand, and our interest in the data on the other hand.

The access.log file follows a format laid out in the accesslog.format configuration option. The contents of this option are included as plain text on each line, but only for entries starting with a percent sign. These entries are placeholders for information about the logged event. Here is a list of these placeholders:

Placeholder	Example Value	Description
%A	ourdomain.com	Our server's address
%a	127.0.0.1	The client's IP address
%B, %b	12756	Bytes sent for the body
%f	/var/www/index.html	The physical filename sent
%H	HTTP/1.1	HTTP protocol version

Placeholder	Example Value	Description
%h	otherdomain.com	Client domain name (or IP address if DNS lookup failed)
%I	635	Number of bytes used for the request
%{name}i	/index.html	The request header with the name given in curly braces. Example: %{Referer}i
%m	GET	The request method (GET, POST, and so on.)
%O	13242	Number of bytes sent for the whole response (headers + body)
%{name}o	12756	The response header with the name given in curly braces. Example: %{Content-Length}o
%p	80	The port on which the request was received
%q	lang=en	The query string (GET parameters)
%r	GET /index.html HTTP/1.1	The request line (method, URI, protocol)
%s, %>s, %<s	200	The returned status code (other notations for Apache compatibility)
%T	2	Time in seconds used for the request
%t	11/Jan/2008:11:11:11 +0100	A time stamp for the request
%U	/index.html	The requested URI
%u	andre	The authenticated user or "-" if the user is not authenticated
%V	sub.ourdomain.com	Host name of the request
%v	ourdomain.com	Host name of our Lighttpd (server.name)
%X	+	A "+" for keep-alive requests, else "-"
%%	%	Adds a percent sign

The default for `accesslog.format` is `"%h %l %u %t \"%r\" %>s %b \"%{Referer}i\" \"%{User-Agent}i\""` in compliance with the CLF. The other configuration options of `mod_accesslog` allow us to use a syslog daemon for logging or specifying an alternative file path for the access log:

```
# either
accesslog.use-syslog = "enable"
# or
accesslog.filename = "/var/log/lighttpd.log"
```

Tracking Users

Many sites use unique cookies to track users. There are two use cases for them: first, we may want to know how the users access our site "clickstream", second, we could have a web application that uses the cookies as a key into an internal session table.

Never use cookies as a single session key

If we use cookies as session keys, we should always add a check for the client IP address before permitting session access. Otherwise, our site could allow session-stealing attacks, even if the cookies are hard to guess.

The idiom is so common that Lighttpd has grown a module to do it. The `mod_usertrack` module does nothing but set a cookie so that we can track the users through multiple connections. A sample `mod_usertrack` configuration snippet is here:

```
server.modules += ("mod_usertrack")
usertrack.cookie-domain = "ourdomain.com"
usertrack.cookie-max-age = 3600 # make the cookie last an hour
usertrack.cookie-name = "ourid"
```

This sets the cookie-domain to our domain, makes the cookies last an hour, and gives the cookie a name of "ourid". Note that all settings can be used within selectors (to limit the reach of the cookie, for example, excluding images).

The following table of settings will explain why we should use all three settings if we employ `mod_usertrack` to set session cookies:

Option	Description
usertrack.cookie-domain	This is the domain of the cookie; so the client will send it back only to the servers with this domain. That is why it should be equal to our domain, or we cannot read the cookie. Worse, other servers would also be able to read our cookie.
usertrack.cookie-max-age	If this is not set, the cookies will never expire. This may even be desirable from our point of view, but may alienate some of our users.
usertrack.cookie-name	The name of the cookie defaults to TRACKID. This will be visible to the users who care, so we should use an innocent sounding name. Older Lighttpd versions use `usertrack.cookie-name` instead, which is deprecated in Lighttpd 1.4.

The cookie generated by `mod_usertrack` is an MD5 hash of the URI path, the current time, and a random number.

Two reasons for letting our cookies expire

First, if we use the cookie as a session key, expiring the cookie will expire the session and enhance security (note that a new cookie will be given to the user). Second, some users see their privacy invaded by permanent cookies, and will delete them or even disable them altogether.

Needless to say, we can use the cookie in selectors, mod_magnet scripts and CGI / SCGI / FastCGI applications. The use of selectors will usually be limited to the absence of our cookie, as in the following example:

```
server.modules = (..., "mod_rewrite", ..., "mod_usertrack", ...)
# usertracking as above
$HTTP["cookie"] !~ "ourid=" {
  url.redirect = ("" => "/nocookie.html")
}
```

The user gets redirected to nocookie.html if no cookie is returned. In conjunction with mod_usertrack, the redirect will only be shown to users that disable cookies for our site.

Note that since the cookie is completely random, and even in a hashed form contains no information about the client IP address or other characteristics, most people will not object to this anonymized use of the data, as long as there is no sensitive information in the URIs and their IP addresses are not stored on our server after the expiry of a session (that is, set our accesslog.format to exclude "%h").

Still, there is one small problem in using the access log files for clickstream analysis. Lighttpd does not support logging cookies yet. To solve this, we have two options: first, there is a patch against Lighttpd version 1.5.0 that allows logging cookies with "%{cookie-name}C" in the log pattern. Second, we could use mod_setenv to add the cookie value to the environment before logging, so we can get the value from there.

To enable cookie logging in Lighttpd 1.5.0, we need to download the patch from http://trac.lighttpd.net/trac/raw-attachment/ticket/1145/cookie.log. patch.txt, and save it in the base path of our Lighttpd source directory. Then we can apply the patch with the following command line:

```
$ patch -p0 < cookie.log.patch.txt
patching file src/mod_accesslog.c
patch unexpectedly ends in middle of line
Hunk #3 succeeded at 881 with fuzz 1.
```

Now recompile our Lighttpd and change the `accesslog.format` to include "%C". An explanation of the `mod_accesslog` configuration is given above. For example, we could add the following line to our configuration:

```
server.modules = ("mod_accesslog", ...)

# remove %h (client IP) from log
# add %{ourid}C to get ourid-cookie-value instead
accesslog.format = "%{ourid}C %l %u %t \"%r\" %>s %b \"%{Referer}i\"
\"%{User-Agent}i\""
```

The second option does not involve recompiling Lighttpd. We use `mod_setenv` to put the cookie value into the environment and configure `mod_accesslog` to use the environment value instead of the client IP:

```
server.modules = ("mod_setenv", "mod_accesslog", ...)

$HTTP["cookie"] =~ "ourid=(.{32})" {
   # the above should match our MD5 hash. Now put it into
   # the request
   setenv.add-request-header = ("ourid" => "%1")
}
# uncomment the following lines if you want to use the
# client IP address if cookies are disabled.
# else $HTTP["remoteip"] =~ "(.*)" {
#   setenv.add-request-header = ("ourid" => "%1")
#}

# remove %h (client IP) from log
# add %{ourid}i to get ourid-cookie-value instead
accesslog.format = "%{ourid}i %l %u %t \"%r\" %>s %b \"%{Referer}i\"
\"%{User-Agent}i\""
```

The second method has the advantage of working without a recompile; however, it uses one additional (but small) module. If we are already using `mod_setenv` (for example, to set response headers), we can put it to another use through this method. If not, we may have to decide if we want to invest about half a kilobyte or recompile our Lighttpd.

No matter which way we choose, we should certainly set up our logging to include the `mod_usertrack` cookie instead of client IP, if we are serious about clickstream analysis or the privacy of our users.

Clickstream Analysis: Client IP address vs. Cookies

There is an ongoing discussion whether to use the client IP address or a unique cookie to distinguish unique visitors. Both methods have their upsides and downsides. Client IP addresses may be the same for different visitors (for example, two visitors being behind the same proxy), while cookies may be deactivated by the client. However, if we respect the visitors of our site, we should also respect their privacy.

Other Data Points

By default, a web server gets some data from the client in exchange for its services. The usual HTTP requests come with some headers that are usually not in use, but can give us information about the users. Here is a table of possible interesting HTTP GET headers:

Header Name	Example Value	Description
Accept	*/*, text/html	A list of MIME types the client will accept for a request
Accept-Charset	utf-8,iso-8859-1	A list of character sets and encodings (mostly compression) that the client will accept
Accept-Encoding	*, gzip, compress	
Accept-Language	en-us, en-gb;q=0.2, en	A list of acceptable languages; we could use this as an alternative or in conjunction with `mod_geoip`
Referer	`http://ourdomain.com/`	The site from which the client was directed to the requested site
User-Agent	Mozilla/4.0 (compatible; MSIE 6.0; Windows NT 5.0)	A String containing information about the browser used

We can add any of these header values to our access log by adding `"%{header-name}i"` to the `accesslog.format` option (where the header-name is one of the above header names). Note that only the `Referer` and the `User-Agent` header can be used in a selector (refer to Chapter 2 for an example). All request headers can be used from `mod_magnet` or any of the `*CGI` backends.

The `Referer` header is not sent by all browsers, and those that send it tend to do it only if the `Referer` is from our site (for example, set it when loading images, CSS, and so on to an already loaded HTML page, otherwise omit it entirely).

The User-Agent string can be used to distinguish between different browser brands, but be warned that some browsers try to pass for other brands, because in the early days of the Web, a group of less-than-clever website operators had the stunning idea to allow access to their sites only through one brand of browsers. Luckily, most operators have found out now that this is a bad idea, but the legacy lives on in some browsers (notably Opera).

Summary

We can learn more about our users, and use this information to personalize our site without gathering too much information or using it in an irresponsible manner.

mod_geoip will enable us to assume a user's location. This can be used to present a country-specific site, maybe even translated to the user's presumed language. Of course we should use this only as a default setting and allow our users to override this; otherwise we will invariably end up angering some of them.

Also the module could be used to block specific content for some countries, for example, to comply with national takedown notices.

mod_accesslog can be configured to put the information we want into the access. log while keeping the information we don't want from clogging our disk space.

mod_usertrack allows us to set unique random cookies in an easy standardized way. While we don't have to care about the content of the cookies any more, we should still use them with care, to avoid opening security holes or enraging our privacy-aware users. Patching mod_accesslog, or rewriting the query to include the cookie information allows us to log the cookie to enable the clickstream analysis.

Finally, the HTTP protocol gives us some information on our clients. While the utility of this information is mostly limited to statistics, we might use some of it in conjunction with the other methods.

6
Encryption: SSL

In this chapter, we will learn:

- How to create a self-assigned key
- How to set keys for certificate authority
- How to obtain keys from other suppliers
- How to configure Lighttpd to use SSL

For many applications, you may want to secure the user — web-server transport from eavesdropping and tampering. To solve this problem, the **Secure Socket Layer (SSL)** was created as a transparent layer between the TCP/IP transport and higher protocols using streams. SSL provides authentication and encryption based on Public Key Cryptography.

In short, Public Key Cryptography works with two keys on each side — one for encryption and authentication, which is called a certificate or public key, and the other for decryption and signing, which is called a private key. The public key can be published freely, while the private key has to be kept — well, private. For a more detailed discussion, read:

Introduction to Public Key Cryptography from Sun Microsystems at `http://docs.sun.com/source/816-6154-10/` or RSA crypto FAQ at `http://www.rsa.com/rsalabs/node.asp?id=2152`.

We will not discuss signing here as Lighttpd uses SSL only for encryption and is rarely used anyway. The client will ask the server for its certificate, while giving the server its own. The server can then encrypt the communication with the client's certificate, while the client will encrypt with the certificate of the server. Both use their respective private keys to decrypt the messages.

Keep your private key under tight security, or an attacker will decrypt the client's requests, possibly revealing sensitive information.

Before we can enable SSL in Lighttpd, we need to generate a key pair, or obtain it in some other way. Assuming that we use OpenSSL, we can use the following examples (tested with version 0.98d).

Let's go through the methods, which range from simple to extensive.

Self-Signed Keys

The easiest method for key pair creation is to create a self-signed key. This key is self-signed because no other authority guarantees its authenticity. For testing purposes, it is sufficient to create one that works for **30 days** using the following command:

```
openssl req -new -x509 -keyout server.pem -out server.pem -nodes
```

This command will ask some questions. If you want to use the default, just press **enter**. If you want to leave them blank, you can enter a period. However, the certificate may then be deemed invalid by some clients.

Country Name (2 letter code) [AU]: UK
State or Province Name (full name) [Some-State]: .
Locality Name (eg, city) []: London
Organization Name (eg, company) [Internet Widgits Pty Ltd]: Packt Publishing
Organizational Unit Name (eg, section) []: .
Common Name (eg, YOUR name) []: www.packtpub.com
Email Address []: admin@packtpub.com

Enter country name, city name, organization name and email address. For the common name, enter your server address. The common name will be the full domain name of our server, for example, somedomain.org or other.domain.com.

 To use the certificate for a multitude of subdomains, you may use * as wildcard, for example, *.mydomain.net

After we have answered all the questions, OpenSSL will create a file named `server.pem` which you should store with minimal permissions. Usually, we want to put this file in the same directory where we keep the `lighttpd.conf` file. The encryption file will be secure as long as we keep the file secure, but most browsers on the market will still mark our site as potentially insecure. There is no way to find out if the key really belongs to our server.

We can use this key pair to test out SSL with your Lighttpd. If we do not care about the warnings that browsers emit when loading a page using this key pair, we can use such a key even in production. However, we may want to give it a longer expiry by adding `-days n` (where n is the number of days the key pair is valid, for example, 365 for a year) to the command line.

If a certificate expires, most browsers will give a warning. To renew a certificate and suppress the warning, simply create a new key pair exactly as described earlier.

Being our own Certificate Authority

If we do not want all browsers to worry users with a warning, but we know that our users will trust us enough to install a certificate, it is possible to become our own **Certificate Authority (CA)** using OpenSSL. This is only a little more work than using a self-signed certificate.

OpenSSL includes a demo-CA, but we need to set up a few things to use it. First, go into a clean directory (possibly create it before). Now, create a directory called "demoCA". Then, create a file with the name of "serial" with the string "01" (that is zero-one) in it, plus an empty file called `index.txt`. The following commands will do this on the usual POSIX-compatible system:

```
> mkdir demoCA
> cd demoCA
> mkdir private newcerts
> touch index.txt
> echo 01 > serial
```

Now, set up a key for the CA, similar to the self-signed key described earlier, but with the CA-extensions. OpenSSL will prompt for a password to secure your CA; enter it twice. Then, it will ask the same questions as it does for the self-signed key. Do not leave any field other than the organizational unit empty, or we will run into errors later. Enter the name of your personal CA into the **Common Name** field. For this example, I base my CA in Munich, Germany, as I happen to sit in a train from there while I write this. You will of course want to base your CA where you happen to be.

```
> openssl req -new -x509 -extensions v3_ca -keyout private/cakey.pem
-out cacert.pem -days 365
```

Generating a 1024 bit RSA private key

.......................++++++

.........++++++

writing new private key to 'private/cakey.pem'

Enter PEM pass phrase: [enter the password here silently]

Verifying - Enter PEM pass phrase: [enter the same password again]

You are about to be asked to enter information that will be incorporated

into your certificate request.

What you are about to enter is what is called a Distinguished Name or a DN.

There are quite a few fields but you can leave some blank

For some fields there will be a default value,

If you enter '.', the field will be left blank.

Country Name (2 letter code) [AU]:de

State or Province Name (full name) [Some-State]:Bavaria

Locality Name (eg, city) []:Munich

Organization Name (eg, company) [Internet Widgits Pty Ltd]:MuniCA

Organizational Unit Name (eg, section) []:.

Common Name (eg, YOUR name) []:MuniCA Certificate Authority

Email Address []:test@munica.de

The CA key has been created. Now, go up one directory and create a request with the same data as you would for a self-signed key. OpenSSL will ask the usual questions again. When it comes to the **Common Name**, this time enter the hostname of our server. The optional fields can safely be left empty. However, all other fields must be set, or we will run into errors later.

For our example, we will request a signed key pair for the domain, `lighttpd.` `packtpub.com`. Note that the country code must be the same as that of our CA key pair. However, the country code does not need to correspond to our top-level-domain.

```
> cd..
> openssl req -new -nodes -out req.pem
```

Generating a 1024 bit RSA private key

....++++++

...........................++++++

writing new private key to 'privkey.pem'

You are about to be asked to enter information that will be incorporated

into your certificate request.

What you are about to enter is what is called a Distinguished Name or a DN.

There are quite a few fields but you can leave some blank

For some fields there will be a default value,

If you enter '.', the field will be left blank.

Country Name (2 letter code) [AU]:de

State or Province Name (full name) [Some-State]:Bavaria

Locality Name (eg, city) []:Munich

Organization Name (eg, company) [Internet Widgits Pty Ltd]:MuniCA

Organizational Unit Name (eg, section) []:Lighttpd Testing

Common Name (eg, YOUR name) []:lighttpd.packtpub.com

Email Address []:lighttpd@packtpub.com

Please enter the following 'extra' attributes

to be sent with your certificate request

A challenge password []:

An optional company name []:

Now, we are ready to create a key pair and sign it as the CA in one step. Enter the CA password to sign the certificate created with the data of the request.

> openssl ca -out cert.pem -infiles req.pem

Using configuration from /usr/ssl/openssl.cnf

Enter pass phrase for ./demoCA/private/cakey.pem: [enter the CA password here]

Check that the request matches the signature

Signature ok

Certificate Details:

    Serial Number: 1 (0x1)

    Validity

        Not Before: Jan 11 17:05:13 2007 GMT

        Not After : Jan 11 17:05:13 2008 GMT

    Subject:

countryName	= de
stateOrProvinceName	= Bavaria
organizationName	= MuniCA
commonName	= lighttpd.packtpub.com
emailAddress	= lighttpd@packtpub.com

    X509v3 extensions:

    X509v3 Basic Constraints:

        CA:FALSE

    Netscape Comment:

        OpenSSL Generated Certificate

    X509v3 Subject Key Identifier:

        4E:50:69:57:F0:F2:62:D9:A6:FE:ED:38:E0:1E:06:51:F8:4F:8A:E1

    X509v3 Authority Key Identifier:

        keyid:09:57:68:CB:F3:90:E1:05:88:8A:CD:8B:5C:BD:D4:F1:E2:6A:A7:11

Certificate is to be certified until Jan 11 17:05:13 2008 GMT (365 days)

Sign the certificate? [y/n]:y

1 out of 1 certificate requests certified, commit? [y/n]y

Write out database with 1 new entries

Data Base Updated

If all works well, we have two files now, `cert.pem` and `privkey.pem`. Just join them to our `server.pem` (assuming our Lighttpd config directory is `/etc/lighttpd`):

```
> cat privkey.pem cert.pem > /etc/lighttpd/server.pem
```

We can use this key pair to run Lighttpd. All browsers will still warn us about an unknown CA unless we install our CA certificate. So this key pair will be sufficient for sites with restricted audience.

If we are running a commercial site, our customers will expect us to have a certificate from a known authority.

Obtaining a Key Pair from a Third-Party Supplier

Most commercial CAs will issue short-lived, cost-free certificates for testing purposes. If you have a web browser, you can see the "usual" Certificate Authorities by looking for certificates in the preferences.

With Firefox 2 or 3, click **Tools | Options | Advanced | Encryption |View Certificates | Authorities**.

With Internet Explorer 7, you need to click **Tools | Internet Options | Content | Certificates | Trusted Root Certificate Authorities**.

Certificates signed by these CAs will show up as secure in this browser. Note that while all browsers appear to trust the biggest CAs, some smaller Authorities (for example, StartCom, a company giving out free certificates) will show up only in Firefox, Konqueror and Friends. If we know that most of our users browse our site with one of these, go to `https://cert.startcom.org/?app=101` and get a free certificate from StartCom CA. Otherwise, we will need to spend the cash.

I will not recommend a commercial CA, as any recommendation will get outdated in a few months, given the eventful nature of the Internet. A list of CAs can be found at `http://www.pki-page.org/`.

To request a certificate from a CA, you do not need OpenSSL, as virtually all CAs will have a web-based form to create the request automatically. Most CAs will give detailed explanation on how to get a certificate from them.

Configuring Lighttpd to use SSL

The two configuration entries to use are `ssl.engine` and `ssl.pemfile`. To enable SSL, set `ssl.engine="enable"`; to disable SSL, set `ssl.engine="disable"`.

The `ssl.pemfile` should contain the path of your `server.pem` relative to the configuration file. If we only want to serve HTTPS, we can simply change our `server.port` and enable SSL:

```
server.port = 443                        # standard HTTPS port
ssl.engine = "enable"
ssl.pemfile = "server.pem"
```

Usually we may want to serve HTTP and HTTPS, depending on how the client is connected. Remember selectors from Chapter 2? We can put the following into our configuration:

```
$SERVER["socket"] == ":443" {
    ssl.engine = "enable"
    ssl.pemfile = "server.pem"
}
```

Unless we use $SERVER["socket"] elsewhere, adding this snippet will allow all pages to be requested via HTTP or HTTPS without changing their functionality.

Sometimes, we want to go one step further, and redirect all traffic to HTTPS for a security-conscious subset of our site. We can do this using mod_redirect, which we had discussed in Chapter 2. Here is an example that sets up redirection to HTTPS for one subdomain:

```
$SERVER["socket"] == ":80" {
    $HTTP["host"] == "subdomain.example.org" {
        url-redirect = ("/(.*)" => "https://subdomain.example.org/$1")
    }
}
```

Put it into our configuration in addition to the previous snippet, and all traffic for `http://subdomain.example.org` will automatically be redirected to `https://subdomain.example.org`. If we want to do this for more than one domain (let us assume they all start with "sec" for simplicity), we can use the percent sign capture trick outlined in Chapter 2 as follows:

```
$SERVER["socket"] == ":80" {
    $HTTP["url"] == "(sec.*)\.example\.org/.*" {
            url-redirect = ("/(.*)" => "https://%1.example.org/$1")
    }
}
```

Congratulations, our Lighttpd can now handle encrypted communication!

Summary

If we care about the security of our site, encrypting our traffic should be a no-brainer. The configuration is quite simple. Use `ssl.enable = "enable"` to enable SSL, and `ssl.pemfile` to point to our public or private key pair.

If we can afford to pay for a certificate, there are many options on the market, which will provide optimal security and are trusted by most browsers (and, in effect, users). Otherwise, a self-signed key pair created with `openssl req` is enough to encrypt our traffic.

7
Securing Lighttpd

Until now, we have allowed any user or attacker to read any file below our document-root without boundaries or surveillance. This may include calling our web applications with any conceivable parameter, no matter how long or how strange the characters may be. For many applications, we may want to know or even restrict what users or attackers can do with our Lighttpd, and programs connected to it.

Our goal as administrator is to keep the system running for the lawful users while keeping out attackers as far as possible. The problem is our inability to distinguish between attackers and lawful users, because attackers can use seemingly harmless interactions, while lawful users may occasionally try something stupid.

Attackers will usually try to do one of the following three things:

- Access a resource in huge numbers to overwhelm the server
- Access a resource that they are not privileged to access
- Access a resource in a way that harms the application

To repel attackers, and to make it easier to distinguish them from lawful users, we need to erect some fences.

Barriers to Entry

The simplest version of access control involves unconditionally denying access to certain files. Lighttpd has `mod_access`, which defines a `url.access-deny` directive that gets a list of patterns to look for. If one of these patterns match, Lighttpd will give a 404 (File not Found) error instead of sending the file. Combined with our trustworthy selectors, we can deny access to certain files, to certain remote addresses, to certain browsers, to clients without a certain cookie, or to files not coming from a certain referrer:

```
# deny access to files with a "~" or ".bak" in the name
url.access-deny = ("~", ".bak")
```

By the way, the reason for sending a 404 error is to keep the attacker in the dark if a file that he or she might not access is there or not.

```
# deny access to all files below a certain path
$HTTP["url"] =~ "/certain-path/" { url.access-deny = ("") }

# deny access on all jpeg images to the Google bot
$HTTP["useragent"] =~ "Google" { url.access-deny = (".jpg") }

# deny access by referrer
$HTTP["referrer"] !~ "^($|www.ourhost.com)" {
    url.access-deny = ("")
}
```

If we want to allow access only to a group of users, we need authentication. This is usually done by entering a username and password. Lighttpd has `mod_auth` to implement this feature.

`server.modules`: Order matters

The order of `server.modules` is also the order in which the modules handle the request. So it is necessary to include `mod_auth` before including `mod_cgi` or `mod_proxy`. Otherwise, the request will already be processed before access can be denied.

In the face of rewrites and redirects, `mod_auth` can be called more than once for every request. While a redirect is done in the client, and an authentication may be done before and after the redirect, a rewrite would require only one authentication if `mod_auth` is included in `server.modules` before `mod_rewrite`. In this case, the order is more a matter of taste, as it involves a trade-off between marginal speed improvements and a double authentication which adds another security perimeter.

`mod_auth` implements two authentication methods: **plain** and **digest**. The difference between the two is that with the former, the username and password are sent in plain text, while with the latter method only a salted hash of the password is sent.

Despite sounding like something right out of a bakery, a hash is a value derived by a "hash function" that takes in a stream of values and outputs a distinct value. So, the chances of getting the same output for similar but not equal input is very low, and there is also no chance to guess the input stream from the output value. Salting refers to adding a "salt" value before the input to foil attacks that just replay the hash value to login.

Note that the digest method (as of version 1.4.20) is slightly out of standard, as it still allows a replay attack. The best bet for security is to authenticate only over HTTPS, so that the username and password will not be sent unencrypted.

Let us start with the most simple authentication method. We can use it as follows:

```
server.modules = ( # ...after rewrites, and redirects.
   "mod_auth", # ...before fastcgi, rrdtool, etc.
)
auth.backend = "plain"
auth.backend.plain.userfile = "/etc/lighttpd/lighttpd.users"
auth.require = ( "/membersonly" =>
   (     "method" => "basic",
         "realm" => "Members only",
         "require" => "valid-user" )
)
```

This will require authentication before allowing access to everything below the "members only" directory. The realm will usually show up in the authentication dialog browsers display. The "require" option can also contain a vertical-bar-separated list of users such as "user=me|user=you".

To hold the users and passwords, we create a user file in `/etc/lighttpd/lighttpd.users` with each line containing a username and password, separated by a colon. Empty lines are not allowed. Such a file would look like this:

```
me:secret
you:password
andre:bogus
```

Surely no one would use passwords this weak! Anyway, we can define multiple user files for different areas using selectors:

```
auth.backend = "plain"
$HTTP["host"] == "staff.mydomain.net" {
   auth.backend.plain.userfile = "/etc/lighttpd/staff.users"
   auth.require = ( "/" =>
         (           "method" => "basic",
                     "realm" => "Staff only",
                     "require" => "valid-user"      )
   )
} else $HTTP["host"] == "members.mydomain.net" {
   auth.backend.plain.userfile = "/etc/lighttpd/members.users"
   auth.require = ( "/" =>
         (           "method" => "basic",
                     "realm" => "Members only",
                     "require" => "valid-user"      )
   )
}
```

This example would require a staff and a member user file like the one we created earlier.

The drawback of plain authentication, besides the clear-text sending of passwords, is that anyone with access to the users file can read them in the clear. To make it a little bit harder to obtain passwords this way, we can use digest authentication. Lighttpd implements two hash functions for this method, namely UNIX crypt and MD5. The former maintains userfile compatibility with Apache (and its htpasswd tool), but is cryptographically weak. The latter is much stronger, at the cost of using a different format.

To use the crypt function, we just change the auth block to:

```
auth.backend = "htpasswd"
auth.backend.htpasswd.userfile = "/etc/lighttpd/htpasswd.user"

auth.require = ("/" =>
     (              "method" => "digest,
                    "realm" => "Members only",
                    "require" => "valid-user"   )
     )
```

Now, our `/etc/lighttpd/htpasswd.user` file needs to contain the username and crypted password, for example:

```
me:fSTNkG1MuEWKs
you:R2Xj0BGOvqQyc
andre:cBWFgkg0nbDGk
```

To create such a file, use either the Apache htpasswd tool or the following bash script (presuming our system has a UNIX crypt utility):

```
#!/bin/bash
# htpasswd.sh - create a htpasswd entry
# usage: htpasswd.sh [username] [password]
echo $1:$(crypt $2)
```

Alternatively, the htdigest backend will do MD5 hashing for us. Just change the first two lines of our previous configuration snippet:

```
auth.backend = "htdigest"
auth.backend.htdigest.userfile = "/etc/lighttpd/htdigest.user"
```

The MD5'd `htdigest.user` file needs to contain the realm and would look like this:

```
me:Members only:dc97b661b50d882cea7a3d9041a4651a
you:Members only:5bb0ccec87fafcdd5400dd2e075986eb
andre:Members only:817a7c2ec1700c70f8421ca34d94e0d7
```

To create this file, use the Apache htdigest tool or the following bash script:

```
#!/bin/bash
# htdigest.sh - create a htdigest entry
# usage: htdigest.sh [username] [realm] [password]
echo $1:$2:$(echo $1:$2:$3 | md5sum | cut -b -32)
```

If md5sum is not available on our system, here is an alternative python implementation that runs without it:

```
#!/usr/bin/python
# htdigest.py [user] [realm] [password]
import sys, md5
a = sys.argv
print a[1] + ":" + a[2] + ":" + md5.new(a[1] + a[2] + a[3]).
hexdigest()
```

mod_auth also allows authenticating against an LDAP directory. **LDAP** means **Lightweight Directory Access Protocol** and these directories are used as a phone and address book and may allow authentication against a single source to all applications that use LDAP. This method is recommended if you already have a LDAP directory set up or if you have a large number of users. In the latter case, there are many free and commercial offerings, notably OpenLDAP from http://openldap.org and from http://www.sun.com/software/products/ directory_srvr_ee/get.jsp the Sun Java System Directory Server (formerly iPlanet).

To connect Lighttpd to such an LDAP server, we configure **mod_auth** as such:

```
auth.backend.ldap.hostname = "localhost" # or wherever our LDAP is
auth.backend.ldap.base-dn = "dc=my-domain,dc=com"
auth.backend.ldap.filter = "(uid=$)"

# optional use TLS (needs a CA certificate, see Chapter 4)
auth.backend.ldap.starttls = "enable"
auth.backend.ldap.ca-file = "/etc/lighttpd/CAcert.pem"
```

This will make Lighttpd try to bind and authenticate against the directory every time HTTP authentication is required.

If we do not want to use HTTP authentication, we can use a mod_fastcgi authorizer or a cookie-based authentication. The advice of encrypting the authentication session using HTTPS applies here as well.

Evading Denial of Service Attacks

A **Denial of Service** attack (or short **DoS**) is an attack by which the server is overwhelmed by requests until it exhausts one of the needed resources (like memory or file handles) and stops responding.

This type of attack does not take special skills; any script kiddie can launch one. However, Lighttpd is not easy to overwhelm, and we can make it even harder.

Before we try to evade them, we need to understand how DoS attacks are carried out. The idea is simple: send as many requests as you can to a server. This means the attacker can maximize the strength of the attacks by distributing the task of sending packets. This is the reason many folks try to take over as many computers as possible by sending out internet worms, creating a "bot-net" of lots of compromised machines.

To make things even worse, the attacker will swamp our Lighttpd with lots of request packets containing bogus IP addresses. So our poor Lighttpd will try to send out responses to other servers which are not even listening. This also means that we cannot trace the attacker by the IP addresses of the requests.

Most DoS attacks do not target the HTTP server directly, but the underlying TCP stack or the network layer of the operating system (for example, by sending "ping" requests). This means Lighttpd's immunity against such attacks is limited by the vulnerability of the host system network stack, which is another reason to choose a POSIX-compatible operating system, as they tend to have solid network stacks.

The proliferation of high-profile sites such as `http://slashdot.org` means that a lot of traffic can be induced just by spreading the word to the web server. A "slashdotting" looks quite like a distributed DoS attack. In this case, the clients are interested in our response, but there are so many of them that it is hard to keep up.

The term "slashdotting" is named after the website, `http://slashdot.org`. There are many other sites now. So, if you have a good (or bad) day, your site can be slashdotted, dugg and boingboinged at the same time!

More and more sites today are created dynamically. This allows for great flexibility, but comes at a performance cost—every request has to be touched by Lighttpd, our CGI, SCGI or FastCGI program, and the database we use. This takes away CPU time, memory, file handles and probably some other valuable system resources. So the first thing to do in order to survive a massive number of requests is to **mirror** the most-requested content and route the traffic to the static mirror instead. We might even get away with doing this dynamically if we **cache** dynamically generated content. The cache will keep the most wanted sites, and our CGI or database will not be touched.

However, to control caching, we can use `mod_magnet` as of version 1.4.12. This is a Lighttpd module that wraps **Lua**, a powerful but small scripting language, thereby adding the capacity to change the request and response parameters or even generate the response directly in the Lighttpd process. We will learn more about it in Chapter 12, but here is a small example to whet your appetite:

```
-- let us assume that our application writes temporary files
-- into /var/tmp/lighttpd-cache
local p = "/var/tmp/lighttpd-cache/" .. lighty.env["physical.path"]
if lighty.stat(p) ~= nil then
    output_include = { { filename = p } }
    return 200
else
    return lighty.RESTART_REQUEST
end
```

We could put this in a file named "cache.lua" next to our configuration, to which we add the following:

```
server.modules = ( #...after auth, access, rewrites and redirects,
    "mod_magnet",
    # ... but before the CGI and logging modules
)
magnet.attract-physical-path-to = "cache.lua"
```

We can also limit the caching with selectors:

```
$HTTP["url"] =~ "cgi-bin/" { # only cache the cgi-bin path
    magnet.attract-physical-path-to = "cache.lua"
}
```

The next thing we can do is to limit the number of connections, which as of Lighttpd 1.5.0 can be done with `mod_evasive`. The configuration for `mod_evasive` has only one setting:

```
evasive.max-conns-per-ip = 4          # allows only four concurrent
                                      # connections for one IP
```

For a distributed Denial of Service from an attacker, this will probably not help due to IP spoofing, but it might help survive a slashdotting.

Probably the best weapon against a DoS attack with IP spoofing is the configuration option, `server.max_write_idle`. This option controls how long Lighttpd will try sending out packets if the client is not taking them. The standard value of 360 seconds is way too high in case of a DoS attack. Turning it down to 60 or even 30 seconds will make Lighttpd drop slow connections, but also drop faked connections faster. Depending on our site and requirements, a higher or lower value may work better.

Another knob to turn is HTTP **keepalive** — a feature of HTTP wherein a connection is left open over a series of requests to save the hassle of re-establishing a connection for each new request. The rub is that keepalive improves performance especially if your content is spread over many files, while simultaneously increasing the risk of our Lighttpd maxing out file descriptors. This is because Lighttpd needs a file descriptor for every open connection. If we use CGI or FastCGI, we actually need two, and if we use a database, we might even need three. But this problem has been ameliorated with `mod_magnet`.

Experience has shown that the default values (keepalive for 16 requests, allow idling up to 30 seconds) are quite good for a majority of applications. Again, the problem lies in idling. So, turning down the `server.max-keep-alive-idle` option to 5 or 10 seconds will improve our chances of survival, because file descriptors are recovered quickly. However, this measure increases the chance of closed slow connections. So we should turn this option up again once the attack has waned.

An attacker might try to put a lot of POST requests of ridiculous sizes on your Lighttpd. We can counter this attack by limiting the size of POST requests with the `server.max-request-size` option. Again, we can use selectors to limit the reach of this option — for example, we can have a site for bigger uploads only for authorized users:

```
server.max-request-size = 64 # limit requests to 64k
$HTTP["url"] =~ "/member-area/member-upload.html" {
    server.max-request-size = 524288 # limit requests to 512MB
}
```

The last resource we have to care for is the disk space. An attacker has two ways of filling our disks, through uploaded data or log files. Uploading data requires a web application that can limit the amount of data by IP address and globally. For log files, a responsible administrator will use log rotation and put older logs at another place, compress them or delete them entirely. On BSD, the newsyslog utility performs a similar task.

Setting up Logrotate

The original logrotate apparently comes from RedHat, but there are replacements for almost any system. Most UNIX systems will have packages. Once we have installed it, we need a configuration file (which will usually go into /etc/logrotate.d/, refer to the logrotate manual pages) with something akin to the following:

```
# assuming logs go to /var/log/lighttpd,
# match access.log and error.log
"/var/log/lighttpd/*.log" {
  daily              # rotate at least once per day
  size 10M           # rotate if logfiles grow larger than 10 megabytes
  missingok          # if there is no logfile, that is fine.
  copytruncate       # truncate the logfile and copying instead of moving
  rotate 7           # keep logfiles for 7 days
  mail me@my.org     # mail logfiles to me before they get overwritten
                     # alternatively specify "nomail"
  compress           # grip-compress logfiles to save space
  notifempty         # do not rotate empty logfiles
  sharedscripts      # call script below once per run
  postrotate         # line below called after logs have been rotated
  /etc/init.d/lighttpd reload
                     # should give a SIGHUP to Lighttpd
  endscript          # this ends the postrotate section
}
```

The comments (beginning with "#") should explain our example. The me@my.org mail address is hopefully somewhere secure. We can then start logrotate by hand, which is great for debugging when adding -d to go into debug mode and -f to force rotation:

```
logrotate -d -f
```

Usually a cron job is automatically added by installation. Check the output of crontab -l to ensure this.

Know Your Foe

A good administrator has ways to learn what people do with the system. The primary source of information is the access log, which mod_accesslog will write out. Additionally, Lighttpd writes error logs. These are of special interest, because an attacker will try to provoke errors in order to create system states that circumvent the usual restrictions.

There are many tools that visualize, filter, correlate or otherwise mangle the log entries that a web server emits. Luckily for us, Lighttpd writes it's logs in the standard web server log file format. So tools written for Apache logs will happily munch Lighttpd logs.

RRDtool

RRDtool is probably the easiest way to get a decent visualization of our Lighttpd access logs. **RRD** stands for **Round-Robin Database**, which in this case means that while new data enters the database, old data is discarded.

The neat thing about using RRDtool is that Lighttpd integrates the setup and the data collecting stage with mod_rrdtool. There are only two things to do: install RRDtool and get graphs out of it.

Installing RRDtool is quite easy. There are binary distributions for Windows (with or without Cygwin), AIX, Debian, RedHat and even NetWare on the main download site at http://oss.oetiker.ch/rrdtool/download.en.html. Other Linux distributions have their own packages, for MacOS X, darwinports has a version at http://rrdtool.darwinports.com/.

Even if we do not find a suitable binary install, compiling on a POSIX-like system is quite simple, given that we all have libraries that RRDtool depends on, such as zlib, libpng, freetype, and libart_lgpl. Most Linux systems today have these. We select a build and install the directory. Then we go there and start the compile:

```
$ VERSION = 1.2.17 # change this to match the version we want
$ BUILD_DIR=/tmp/rrdbuild
$ INSTALL_DIR=/usr/
$ mkdir -p $BUILD_DIR && cd $BUILD_DIR
$ # now copy your tar.gz or download, for example using wget:
    --12:34:56-- http://oss.oetiker.ch/rrdtool/pub/rrdtool-.tar.gz
    => 'rrdtool-.tar.gz'
    (... output of wget omitted ...)
$ tar xzf rrdtool-$VERSION.tar.gz
$ cd rrdtool-$VERSION
$ ./configure --prefix=$INSTALL_DIR && make && make install
```

After we have an installed RRDtool, we can set it up to work with our Lighttpd. To do this, we include mod_rrdtool into our lighttpd.conf file:

```
server.modules += ("mod_rrdtool")
rrdtool.binary = "/usr/bin/rrdtool"
rrdtool.db-name = "/var/www/lighttpd.rrd"
```

Now, Lighttpd sets up a Round-Robin Database and fills it with request and traffic data for us. The only thing we still need to do is to extract this data into graphs. This can be done using the `rrdtool-graph.sh` script that comes with the Lighttpd documentation. We just need to change the first three variables to suit our needs.

Starting this script will cause RRDtool to write out some PNG images graphing traffic in bytes per second and requests per second, as shown in the following images:

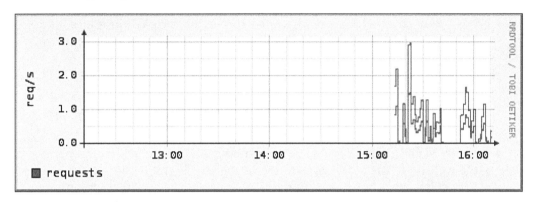

The first graph shows the requests per second while the next shows how many bytes my Lighttpd has pumped out (as you can see, my test server is not exactly overloaded).

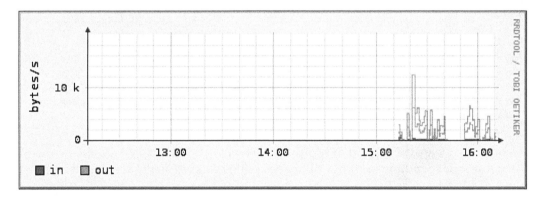

The knowledge of requests and bytes per second allows us to adapt our Lighttpd to the traffic we get. There are other free programs to visualize, parse, or otherwise process the logs. Here is a short lineup:

- The **webalizer** can be downloaded from `http://www.mrunix.net/webalizer` and has a large number of binary packages available from source. Installation is a simple `configure && make && make install`. It does not deal with the timing information and parses the whole logfile (or a date-delimited part of it) to create a chart and a text table with statistics for hits, views, sites, and so on. The webalizer requires the GD graphics library (at `http://www.boutell.com/gd`), which in turn depends on `libpng` and `zlib`, both of which are usually available.

- **AWStats**, another free log mining program written in PERL, so do not expect binary packages. Apart from being run on the command line, it also has a CGI mode (which we will test in Chapter 11). It creates very comprehensive statistics. You can find it at `http://awstats.sf.net`.

- Under `http://www.analog.cx`, we can find **Analog**, which according to the website is "the most popular logfile analyser in the world". It also creates very extensive reports including traffic by date, browser, file types, files, search queries, status codes, and more. Binary packages are provided for a lot of systems.

>
> **We can process logs anywhere**
> Note that the three tools introduced earlier can be used as command line programs. If we use log rotation, we can analyze the mailed log files instead of the files on the server, thereby freeing our server from the resulting load.

Now, we have enough tools at our disposal to see how crowded our server really is. The more interesting thing to do, security-wise, is to look out for unusual patterns. Unfortunately, a computer is bad at finding them, and visualizations often hide important information about a request for the sake of a cleaner picture. Humans, on the other hand, are quite good at spotting unusual things in a stream of information. Therefore, a lot of administrators still regard plain old **grep** as the best log analysis tool available, because it allows us to reduce the information by exclusion. A good procedure is to first use an analyzer to look at the big picture, and then to use grep to get to the details.

Grepping the Logs

grep is one of those utilities that come in handy in unexpected places. It can filter a stream of lines (for example, server logs) for plain text patterns or regular expressions. If we add `-P` to the command line, newer greps will use the same regular expression syntax that Lighttpd uses for selectors, rewrite rules, and so on (refer to Chapter 2). Otherwise, a reduced regular expression language may be used. Check the documentation (for example, man page) of your grep version.

To see what we have to look for, we will just walk through a simple example. While it may be interesting to know which files were served, the files which were not served are quite an amusement, too. For example, we can search our log file (in this case, we search `/var/log/lighttpd/access.log`) for file not found errors using `grep` to filter, and `less` to view, as shown in the following command line:

```
grep ' 404 ' /var/log/lighttpd/access.log | less
```

Or, if we have gzipped our logfile (some systems also have a `gzcat` utility that does the same as `gunzip -c`, namely writing the unpacked contents to standard output):

```
gunzip -c /var/log/lighttpd/access.log.1.gz | grep ' 404 ' | less
```

This shows a simple usage of `grep` with a pattern and a file. Note the spaces between the apostrophes and the 404. Without them, we would get all requests which contain the string "404".

 grep is also available for Windows. Download it at
`http://gnuwin32.sourceforge.net/packages/grep.htm`.

If our server has run for a while, it will show the following lines (IP addresses masked to protect the guilty and my server):

4?.??.??.?? ??.??.??.?2 - [15/Jan/2008:21:23:43 +0100] "GET /phpchat//chat/messagesL.php3 HTTP/1.1" 404 345 "-" "Mozilla/4.0 (compatible; MSIE 6.0; Windows 98)"

2?.??.??.??? ??.??.??.?2 - [17/Jan/2008:21:27:24 +0100] "GET /phpmyadmin/read_dump.phpmain.php HTTP/1.0" 404 345 "-" "-"

6?.??.???.? ??.??.??.?2 - [20/Feb/2008:22:09:44 +0100] "GET //blogs/xmlrpc.php HTTP/1.1" 404 345 "-" "Mozilla/4.0 (compatible; MSIE 6.0; Windows 98)"

1??.??.???.?? ??.??.??.?2 - [31/Mar/2008:21:55:52 +0100] "GET /cacti//graph_image.php HTTP/1.1" 404 345 "-" "Mozilla/4.0 (compatible; MSIE 6.0; Windows 98)"

These are presumably script kiddies or automated hacking tools searching for vulnerable applications — at least I have none of these applications running. Other lines might contain spelling mistakes. Other interesting status codes include 403, 413, 500, and 502. A list of HTTP status codes is in Appendix A.

Apart from `-P`, most grep versions allow the following parameters:

Parameter	Description
`-r`	Recurse into subdirectories, as in grep -r stupid_variable code/
`-i`	Match case insensitivity
`-m [number]`	Match up to [number] lines
`-n`	Prefix matches by line number
`-v`	Inverts match; shows all lines that do not match the pattern
`-o`	Outputs only the matching part instead of the whole line
`-e`	Uses extended regular expressions for matching (though newer versions of grep no longer make any difference)

Invocations of grep can be chained by pipes (with "|", see above) to construct multiple-stage filters. For anything more sophisticated, pulling the logs into a database and using specialized data mining tools is probably the way to go.

The error log can also say some interesting things to us, depending on the log level. Most errors of web applications will end up here. Each error log line consists of a timestamp (as in "`2008-06-11 16:43:40:`"), the source file and a line in parenthesis (like `mod_fastcgi.c.2592` for errors in CGI scripts served through FastCGI) and the actual error message. Messages in `connections.c` correspond to erroneous HTTP(S) requests. If they do not arrive in bulk, they usually do not cause any problem. Messages from `log.c` tell us when the server was stopped, started or reconfigured. A usual error log may have one of the following typical messages:

2008-02-21 18:12:53: (log.c.75) server started

2008-02-21 18:12:56: (mod_fastcgi.c.2570) FastCGI-stderr: ./index.cgi:syntax error [...]

2008-02-24 02:56:28: (request.c.535) no uri specified -> 400

2008-02-27 16:51:55: (connections.c.279) SSL: 1 error:140780E5:SSL routines:SSL23_READ:ssl handshake failure

Depending on whether you serve applications or large files, we may get other log entries. We can specify the parts of the system that we want to log using the following variables:

Configuration entry	Description
`debug.log-condition-cache-handling`	Logs condition cache handling internals for debugging
`debug.log-condition-handling`	Logs condition handling internals for debugging
`debug.log-file-not-found`	Logs every 404 file not found error
`debug.log-request-handling`	Logs request handling internals for debugging
`debug.log-request-header`	Logs each request header
`debug.log-request-header-on-error`	Logs only those request headers that resulted in an error
`debug.log-response-header`	Logs response headers
`debug.log-state-handling`	Logs state handling internals for debugging
`debug.log-timing`	Shows timing information, which is useful for profiling

Summary

The Internet is an insecure space. Therefore we should keep an eye on our server — the logs tell us what we need to know, if we know where to look. Sometimes it is nice to have statistics. We can gather them easily with RRDtool and `mod_rrdtool`.

We can disallow access to certain areas of our site with `mod_access`, and mark out private space where only authenticated users can roam with `mod_auth`. By design, Lighttpd is quite capable of holding on in a Denial of Service or slashdotting. We can harden it further against such "attacks" by changing timeouts and limiting traffic, request sizes and HTTP sessions. Keeping an eye on our resource usage always helps.

Remember that none of the above will help us if we deploy an insecure web application through Lighttpd. The system is only as secure as its weakest part.

8
Containing Lighttpd

In this chapter, we will learn about:

- Mechanisms in Lighttpd that contain attack risks:
    - Giving up privileges
    - Changing roots

- Techniques to implement security

Securing Lighttpd against attacks is a good cause, but there may be attacks of the types we are not even aware of. Under POSIX-like systems, Lighttpd has to run as root, so that it can bind to port 80. This makes it a target worth attacking. Moreover, Lighttpd presents an open interface to the network, so it is easy to try and subvert it.

Attackers will try the most unlikely things to get a system out of the defined states, say, through huge requests with null characters and other niceties. I would not bet my life on the non-existence of a certain request that makes Lighttpd open its doors to an attacker. Therefore, it makes sense to contain the risk to Lighttpd.

Think of a car — it has break assistance, ESP and other "active security" to reduce the likelihood of an accident. But it also has seat belts and airbags to reduce the harm in case an accident happens anyway.

We can do the same with Lighttpd — secure it, so it will not be compromised. But we also need to secure the system from Lighttpd, so that breaking Lighttpd does not break our system.

Lighttpd implements two mechanisms to contain the risk of attack: giving up privileges and changing root. The former method is quite simple and should offer reasonable protection for a normal site. The latter method will restrict hackers to access only the files needed for running Lighttpd, thus granting maximum security.

Note that neither method harms performance.

Giving up Privileges

I must admit that I lied a little when I told you that Lighttpd needs to run with root privileges — the only thing requiring them is binding to Port 80. After binding, Lighttpd can change the user, thus giving up privileges and making it a lesser target for attack. The configuration is so simple that most installation packages enable it by default:

```
server.username = "lighttpd"
server.groupname = "lighttpd"
```

This will make Lighttpd run as user lighttpd in the group lighttpd. The only thing we have to care about is that all of the files we want to serve need to be accessible, and all web applications we want to spawn need to be executable to this user or group.

It's so easy, that there is little reason not to do it. In fact, we may need to do nothing at all, because most installations do it for us by default. Just look into our `lighttpd.conf` file to see if the above statements, possibly with other user and group name, are there and not commented out.

No user or group — no Lighttpd
Make sure that the user and group we want Lighttpd to assume exist on our system. If not, add them with the `groupadd` and `useradd`, respectively before running Lighttpd.

The only reason to keep Lighttpd running as root is that we may want to use per-user directories without requiring the directories to be made readable by the Lighttpd user. However, serving potentially compromised scripts as the root user is a security disaster waiting to happen.

A far more radical approach of separating Lighttpd from the rest of the system is to change the Lighttpd processes' root directory to **chroot**, as it is called in UNIX slang. Note that chroot is only available on UNIX-like systems (this includes MacOS X and cygwin, though I would not recommend running a production server on the latter).

Changing Root

The idea of changing root is that of running security-critical applications in a minimal environment so that an attacker who manages to subvert the application has limited access only to the chroot environment and can use only the tools that this environment supplies.

As with all ideas to improve security, chrooting presents its own share of security problems. If a user gains root privileges, she can break out of a chroot environment by either remounting the file system or `chdir()` out of the chroot until the original root is reached, and then chroot to this directory. So we should configure our Lighttpd to give up root privileges in addition to changing root, and also be sure not to have any User ID executable in our chroot environment.

Set **User ID (SUID** for short) is a method to run a process under a different user's privileges. UNIX file systems allow setting up a SetUID flag on an executable combined with a User ID. The program will be executed with the privileges of the User whose User ID is set. This is useful for programs that need to run with higher privileges (such as Lighttpd), but can be a terrible security issue, as an attacker who subverts a SUID program can gain the privileges of the SUID user.

Keep your chroot environment's `bin/` and `lib/` directories non-writable to any user other than the root user!

Or give me your keys, bank account number, and all of your belongings.☺

Ironically, the biggest threat to chroot security comes from outside the environment. If a user can modify the contents of the chroot environment, she could subvert the environment's libraries to gain root privileges inside the chroot environment. Then she could enter the chroot environment, use the root privileges to break out of the chroot and have total control over the system!

Now that we are sufficiently warned, let's go and build our chroot environment. First, we need a directory to put it. Let us name it `lighttpd`:

```
mkdir /lighttpd
cd /lighttpd
```

Next, we need to create subdirectories for logging in, temporary files, cache, configuration, binary, libraries, and document root:

```
mkdir -p var/log/lighttpd
chown lighttpd:lighttpd var/log/lighttpd
mkdir tmp
chmod 1777 tmp
mkdir -p var/tmp/lighttpd/cache/compress
```

```
chown lighttpd:lighttpd var/tmp/lighttpd/cache/compress
mkdir -p etc/lighttpd
mkdir -p usr/sbin
mkdir -p usr/lib
mkdir -p docroot
chown lighttpd:lighttpd docroot
chmod 0700 docroot
```

Now, we have two options:

- To re-install Lighttpd into the chroot environment use the following command:

  ```
  configure –prefix /lighttpd/usr
  ```

- To copy over the files from the standard environment. The problem here is that we also need to copy the shared libraries. The program ldd can help us find out. Here is a little bash script to automatically copy the necessary shared libraries (you can download the cpdynlib.sh file from : http://www.packtpub.com/files/code/2103_Code.zip).

```bash
#!/bin/bash
# Change FILES according to your system, some systems name the
# library files different than .so - ls /usr/lib/mod* may help.
FILES="/usr/sbin/lighttpd /usr/lib/mod_*.so"for FILE in $FILES
do
    mkdir -p /lighttpd${FILE%/*}
    cp $FILE /lighttpd$FILE
    ldd $FILE | while read A B C D
    do
        # check if there is an entry
        if [ "not" == "$A" ]
        then
                echo "$FILE: not a dynamic executable"
        elif [ -z $C ]
        then
                mkdir -p /lighttpd${A%/*}
                cp $A /lighttpd$A
        else
                mkdir -p /lighttpd${C%/*}
                cp $C /lighttpd$C
        fi
    done
done
```

Finally, we need to copy the SSL certificate into /lighttpd/etc/lighttpd, if we use SSL. Note that the configuration file is read before changing the root. So, we can leave it as is, but for one line:

```
server.chroot = "/lighttpd"
```

The same script can be modified to copy any needed CGI backend into our chroot environment. Just change the first line to make the files point to the executable (if there are any) and the modules, and run it.

Our environment will probably look like the following, although our mileage may vary:

```
$ cd /lighttpd && find . -type f
./etc/lighttpd/lighttpd.pem
./usr/sbin/lighttpd
./usr/lib/libgssapi_krb5.so.2
./usr/lib/libkrb5.so.3
./usr/lib/libk5crypto.so.3
./usr/lib/libz.so.1
./usr/lib/libbz2.so.1
./usr/lib/mod_access.so
... (skipped all the modules for brevity)
./usr/lib/mod_webdav.so
./lib/libpcre.so.0
./lib/libdl.so.2
./lib/libssl.so.4
./lib/libcrypto.so.4
./lib/tls/libc.so.6
./lib/tls/libm.so.6
./lib/ld-linux.so.2
./lib/libcom_err.so.2
./lib/libresolv.so.2
./lib/libcrypt.so.1

$ _
```

Restart Lighttpd. Congratulations, we just got our own chrooted Lighttpd! Now, let us go and copy all the files we want to serve into our /lighttpd/docroot, so that our chrooted Lighttpd will find them.

How to handle errors

Sometimes, ldd will not catch all the dependencies, and our chrooted Lighttpd will crash. To resolve this issue, get a strace utility (Solaris 10 users could also use ptrace). With this utility, we can trace Lighttpd calling the following command:

```
strace /usr/sbin/lighttpd -D -f /etc/lighttpd/lighttpd.conf
```

This will throw up lots of information on the system calls done. We probably need to look only at the last lines before the crash. The last line containing "open", and a filename may be informative, because chances are that filename belongs to the missing file responsible for the crash.

Now, we can add a scripting language and a database to our chroot environment. There is a third way of preparing the chroot environment for some distributions — the package manager might give out a list of files for each package, so we could use this list to copy the files with a little shell magic.

For example, we could call the package manager like this:

```
# for rpm-using distributions, e.g. RedHat, CentOS, Fedora, SuSE, etc.
rpm -q --filesbypkg lighttpd | while read x y; do # x == "lighttpd"
if [! -d $y ]; then cp $y /lighttpd$y; fi
done
# for debian-inspired systems using dpkg
dpkg -L lighttpd | while read x; do
if [! -d $x ]; then cp $x /lighttpd$x; fi
done
# or apt - "apt-file list" is the same as "dpkg -L"
apt-file list lighttpd | while read x; do
if [! -d $x ]; then cp $x /lighttpd$x; fi
done
```

This way, we can copy all the files of a package into our chroot environment. Depending on our distribution, we might need to add additional packages that our Lighttpd package depends on.

 Beware of Missing Files!

Note that using the above method does not necessarily copy all dependencies such as the ldd script mentioned earlier. Also note that the package might contain start/stop scripts and other things that we do not need in the chroot environment. So the ldd method is preferred.

The ldd script above can easily be changed to move the backend. Note that the spawn-FCGI utility used to start backend processes provided with Lighttpd can remain outside the chroot environment, as it is capable of changing root while running. Just edit the first line of our script to make it copy the backend files:

```
# add magnet
FILES="/usr/local/bin/magnet"
# or python (for example 2.4)
FILES="/usr/bin/python $(find /usr/lib/python2.4 -type f)"
# or php-fcgi
FILES="/usr/local/bin/php /etc/php.ini /etc/php.d/*"
```

Running the changed script will copy the selected backend into our chroot environment. This enables us to run dynamic web applications from a chrooted Lighttpd. So even if an attacker could gain privileges through the backend, he or she is stuck in the chroot environment. However, there is an alternative that promises better security.

Separating the Backend

If we use Lighttpd to serve web applications, we may use an external spawner for our application instead of letting Lighttpd spawn the backend processes. This spawner and the needed runtime can be put in a separate chroot environment.

Keeping the backend separate allows us to spawn it under different user privileges or even in a different chroot environment. This reduces the privileges the Lighttpd server needs at the cost of some convenience and perhaps even some avenues for optimization. (For example, `X-Lighttpd-send-file`, requires a path that both environments can read or write, thereby undermining the security of both the environments).

Note that if we need access to static files from the backend, we must copy or link them into both the environments. The first is a hassle, and introduces the risk of having different versions of the same file in each backend. The second negates the effect of separating both the environments. Thus, if we really cannot do without accessing files which are otherwise served directly from Lighttpd, we better use one chroot environment for both Lighttpd and the backend.

If we keep Lighttpd in a chroot environment, keeping the backend out of the environment can drastically reduce the environment size and make it easier to create and manage the chroot environment.

Often the backend is far more complex than Lighttpd, especially with today's Web 2.0 applications. So it may make sense to keep it separate from Lighttpd.

In our example, we will create a user and group called "backend", and make it own all backend files by typing `chown -r backend:backend /backend` into the shell.

We can change the script for our backend, replacing `/lighttpd` with `/backend`, to have a script that moves our backend to a different location. We can now make the backend application listen to a port. But that would potentially open it up to attackers from outside.

There is a final trick we can pull out of our hat to connect both the environments without needing to use a firewall or risk putting our backend online, and that is a FIFO, also called a named pipe. The abbreviation **FIFO** is short for **First In First Out**, which is a succinct and fitting description of a **Queue**.

Lighttpd accepts backend addresses as IPv4, IPv6, ports, and local filenames. This local filename needs to point to a FIFO. The `mkfifo` command can create one for us. To make it appear in both the environments, we can use a hard link. For example:

```
# create a FIFO in our lighttpd chroot environment
mkfifo /lighttpd/etc/backend.socket
```

```
# make our lighttpd user/group own the fifo to get access
chown lighttpd:lighttpd /lighttpd/etc/backend.socket
```

```
# create a hard link into our backend environment
ln /lighttpd/etc/backend.socket /backend/etc/lighttpd.socket
```

```
# make our backend user/group own the linked fifo to get access
chown backend:backend /backend/etc/lighttpd.socket
```

We can use the spawn-FCGI program supplied with Lighttpd (this is why we copied it over with the backend before) to make the backend listen to the socket. The syntax is as follows: `/usr/local/bin/spawn-fcgi -f <executable> -s <socket>`

For example, we can use the Lua magnet:

```
$ /usr/local/bin/spawn-fcgi -f /usr/local/bin/magnet -s \
/etc/lighttpd.socket -u backend -g backend -c backend
```

This will run the Lua magnet in our backend. The spawn-FCGI executable takes the following parameters:

Parameter	Description
-f *<path>*	Indicates the path to the executable file of the FastCGI application; for example, `/usr/local/bin/php` or `/usr/bin/python`
-s *<socket>* -p *<port>*	Indicates the path to a named pipe created with `mkfifo`; a port number that will be listened to
-c *<path>*	(Use a small C here!) Indicates the root of our chroot environment, if the executable is to be chrooted
-u *<username>*	Indicates the user under whose privileges the executable is run
-g *<groupname>*	Indicates the group under whose privileges the executable is run
-C *<number>*	(Use a big C here!) Indicates the number of processes to be spawned

If we use -C to spawn multiple instances of our backend, the spawn-FCGI program will automatically create FIFOs for each instance. For example, we could add -C 2 to our command line, as shown here:

```
$ /usr/local/bin/spawn-fcgi -f /usr/local/bin/magnet -s \
/etc/lighttpd.socket -u backend -g backend -c backend -C 2
```

The spawn-FCGI would then create two files:

```
$ ls /backend/etc/lighttpd.socket*
/backend/etc/lighttpd.socket-0    /backend/etc/lighttpd.socket-1
```

We can now link the sockets into our Lighttpd chroot environment using the following bash commands:

```
$ for name in $(ls /backend/etc/lighttpd.socket*); do
> target=/lighttpd/etc/backend${name#/backend/etc/lighttpd}
> ln $name $target
> chown lighttpd:lighttpd $target
> done
```

Now, the sockets can be accessed from Lighttpd while keeping it separated from the backend. To do this, we need the following in our `lighttpd.conf`. In 1.4 style:

```
fastcgi.server = ("lua" =>
    (
            "backend-0" => ("socket" => "/etc/backend.socket-0", ...),
            "backend-1" => ("socket" => "/etc/backend.socket-1", ...)
    )
)
```

Or in 1.5 style:

```
$HTTP["URL"] =~ "^\.lua" {
    proxy-core.backends = ( # a list of backends
            "/etc/backend.socket-0", "/etc/backend-socket-1")
    ...
}
```

Refer to Chapter 3, Chapter 11, or Appendix B for further information regarding the FastCGI configuration.

To summarize:

1. Start the backends using spawn-FCGI.

2. Link the FIFOs into our Lighttpd chroot environment using the given commands.

3. Start Lighttpd.

Finally, we can go through those three steps and congratulate ourselves on having our Lighttpd and backend fully contained.

Summary

Lighttpd can be run quite securely, if we invest a little in its security. We can use the built-in methods to achieve the least privilege, and hence the highest security.

The least we should do is configure Lighttpd so that it will give up root privileges after binding to the needed ports.

If our site is a high-profile site and/or handles monetary transactions or sensitive user information, we should go all the way and put Lighttpd into a chroot environment. In doing so, we need to be very careful not to create any new entry points for attack.

Putting the backend in a separate environment and keeping only a FIFO open to connect both the environments can introduce another considerable barrier for hackers. This way, at least the backend is cleanly cut off from the outside as well as from the static files. So, attacks that require interferences between both are diverted.

Finally, a small table of pros and cons for both methods:

	Changing User / Group	Running in Chroot Environment
Pro	Easy to achieve	Maximal security, if carefully executed
	A successful attack on Lighttpd gives only user privileges	Allows clean separation from the backend
		Even if an attacker breaks into Lighttpd, he or she is still trapped in the chroot environment
Con	A successful attack on Lighttpd allows the attacker to roam around large portions of the system	Creating a chroot environment is a complex task
	The files to be served need to be accessible to Lighttpd user, so that per-user directories can be made readable to the Lighttpd group	Errors in creating the chroot environment could open fatal holes in the system security
		All files to be served need to be within the chroot environment. Allowing anyone to place files there constitutes a security breach!

9
Optimizing Lighttpd

Lighttpd was introduced at the beginning of this book as a lean and fast web server. This chapter will help us make Lighttpd work even faster. Before we start optimizing our Lighttpd installation, there are some things to consider such as where is Lighttpd going to run?

The most tested system with perhaps the most optimized backend is Linux. So if we need to squeeze every little request per second out of a server, it is a sure guess. In fact, apart from Linux, all systems except Windows are quite capable of delivering good performance.

If our Lighttpd runs on a multi-processor machine, it can take advantage of that by spawning multiple versions of itself. Also, most Lighttpd installations will not have a machine to themselves; therefore, we should not only measure the speed but also its resource usage.

Optimizing Compilers

gcc with the usual settings (-O2) already does quite a good job of creating a fast Lighttpd executable. However, -O3 may nudge the speed up a tiny little bit (or slow it down, depending on our system) at the cost of a bigger executable system. If there are **optimizing compilers** for our platform (for example, Intel and Sun Microsystems each have compilers that optimize for their CPUs), they might even give another tiny speed boost.

If we do not want to invest money in commercial compilers, but maximize on what gcc has to offer, we can use **Acovea**, which is an open source project that employs genetic algorithms and trial-and-error to find the best individual settings for gcc on our platform.

Get it from `http://www.coyotegulch.com/products/acovea/`.

Finally, optimization should stop where security (or, to a lesser extent, maintainability) is compromised. A slower web server that does what we want is way better than a fast web server obeying the commands of a script kiddie.

Before we optimize away blindly, we better have a way to measure the "speed". A useful measure most administrators will agree with is "served requests per second". http_load is a tool to measure the requests per second. We can get it from http://www.acme.com/software/http_load/.

http_load is very simple. Give it a site to request, and it will flood the site with requests, measuring how many are served in a given amount of time. This allows a very simplistic approach to optimizing Lighttpd: Tweak some settings, run http_load with a sufficient realistic scenario, and see if our Lighttpd handles more or less requests than before.

We do not yet know where to spend time optimizing. For this, we need to make use of timing log instrumentation that has been included with Lighttpd 1.5.0 or even use a profiler to see where the most time is spent. However, there are some "big knobs" to turn that can increase performance, where http_load will help us find a good setting.

Installing http_load

http_load can be downloaded as a source .tar file (which was named .tar.gz for me, though it is not gzipped). The version as of this writing is 12Mar2006. Unpack it to /usr/src (or another path by changing the /usr/src) with:

```
$ cd /usr/src && tar xf /path/to/http_load-12Mar2006.tar.gz
$ cd http_load-12Mar2006
```

We can optionally add SSL support. We may skip this if we do not need it.

To add SSL support we need to find out where the SSL libs and includes are. I assume they are in /usr/lib and /usr/include, respectively, but they may or may not be the same on your system. Additionally, there is a "SSL tree" directory that is usually in /usr/ssl or /usr/local/ssl and contains certificates, revocation lists, and so on. Open the Makefile with a text editor and look at line 11 to 14, which reads:

```
#SSL_TREE = /usr/local/ssl
#SSL_DEFS = -DUSE_SSL
#SSL_INC = -I$(SSL_TREE)/include
#SSL_LIBS = -L$(SSL_TREE)/lib -lssl -lcrypto
```

Change them to the following (assuming the given directories are correct):

```
SSL_TREE = /usr/ssl
SSL_DEFS = -DUSE_SSL
SSL_INC = -I/usr/include
SSL_LIBS = -L/usr/lib -lssl -lcrypto
```

 Read on here if you skipped SSL support.

Now compile and install `http_load` with the following command:

$ make all install

Now we're all set to load-test our Lighttpd.

Running http_load Tests

We just need a URL file, which contains URLs that lead to the pages our Lighttpd serves. `http_load` will then fetch these pages at random as long as, or as often as we ask it to. For example, we may have a front page with links to different articles. We can just start putting a link to our front page into the URL file, which we will name `urls` to get started; for example, `http://localhost/index.html`.

Note that the file just contains URLs, nothing less, nothing more (for example, `http_load` does not support blank lines). Now we can make our first test run:

$ http_load -parallel 10 -seconds 60 urls

This will run for one minute and try to open 10 connections per second. Let's see if our Lighttpd keeps up:

```
343 fetches, 10 max parallel, 26814 bytes, in 60 seconds

78.1749 mean bytes/connection

5.71667 fetches/sec, 446.9 bytes/sec

msecs/connect: 290.847 mean, 9094 max, 15 min

msecs/first-response: 181.902 mean, 9016 max, 15 min

HTTP response codes:
  code 200 -- 327
```

As we can see, it does. http_load needs one of the two start conditions and one of the two stop conditions plus a URL file to run. We can create the URL file manually or crawl our document root(s) with the following python script called crawl.py:

```python
#!/usr/bin/python
#run from document root, pipe into URLs file. For example:
# /path/to/docroot$ crawl.py > urls
import os, re, sys

hostname = "http://localhost/"

for (root, dirs, files) in os.walk("."):
  for name in files:
    filepath = os.path.join(root, name)
    print re.sub("\\./", hostname, filepath)
```

You can download the crawl.oy file from
http://www.packtpub.com/files/code/2103_Code.zip.

Capture the output into a file to use as URL file. For example, start the script from within our document root with:

$ python crawl.py > urls

This will give us a urls file, which will make http_load try to get all files (given that we have specified enough requests). Then we can start http_load as discussed in the preceding example. http_load takes the following options:

Option	Useful value	Description
Required start condition		
-rate	100	Try to start the given number of new connections per second. Use a high value to see how high we can ramp up the load.
-parallel	100	Keep the given number of connections open at any given moment, which will work unless Lighttpd is so fast that http_load cannot keep up.
Required stop condition		
-seconds	300	Keep up the load for the given time in seconds.
-fetches	10000	Amass the given number of requests.
Optional arguments		
-verbose		Output stats every minute (for longer test runs).
-proxy	proxy.net:81	Use the proxy specified by the host name and the port.
-timeout	60	Time-out every request after the given seconds (defaults to 60).

Option	Useful value	Description
-cipher (If SSL is enabled)	fastsec	This selects the TLS cipher, for https addresses. We can use one of three keywords or a cipher name. The keywords are: fastsec (RC4-MD5), highsec (DES-CBC3-SHA), and paranoid (AES256-SHA). The SSL main page for ciphers has a list of all the cipher names.
-jitter		If -rate was specified as the start condition, randomly deviates up to ±10% from the given rate.
-throttle		Simulates access by modem users (33.6kbps).
-sip	ips	Selects a random IP address from the file ips (one IP address per line) to use as source address. See below.

For the -sip option, we will need a list of IP addresses. Here is a useful python script that will write a number of distinct IP addresses below a given subnet (which we can then route to our loopback device):

```python
#!/bin/env python
# run with: makeips.py 1000 101.202.0.0
# to create 1000 ip entries in the subnet 101.202.*.*
import random, sys

ips = {}

def makeip(subnet, ip=None):
  while ip is None or ips.get(ip):
    ip = ".".join(x != "0" and x or str(int(random.random()*256))
        for x in subnet.split("."))
  ips[ip] = 1
  return ip

def makeips(amount, subnet):
  maxips = 256 ** sum("0" == x for x in subnet.split("."))
  if maxips < amount:
    print "Can only fit %i ips in the subnet %s." % (maxips, subnet)
    amount = maxips
  ipfile = open("ips", "w")
  for i in xrange(amount):
    ipfile.write(makeip(subnet) + "\n")
  ipfile.close();

if __name__ == "__main__":
  try: makeips(argv[1], argv[2])
  except: print "usage: python makeips.py [amount] [subnet]"
```

You can download the makeips.py code file at http://www.packtpub.com/files/code/2103_Code.zip.

With this we can route the subnet to the loopback device and make it look as if different clients are requesting the pages. Use this to counter the effect of expiry on our tests; as the only alternative would be to remove `mod_expire` from the configuration, which is probably not desirable.

Route a whole subnet to our local host or use one we already have

With UNIX-like operating systems (Linux, Solaris, BSD, and MacOS X), use the `route add` command. On Windows (with or without cygwin), we can make use of the fact that the whole 127.*.*.* network is looped back (using the default IP 127.0.0.1). So running `python makeips.py 255 127.0.0.0` will give us a range of IP addresses we can use even if we cannot change our routing tables.

Before we work on fine tuning our network, we can tweak some configuration settings to increase performance:

1. Select the best event handler and write the backend for the job. Here is the recommendation per system:

System	Linux 2.6	Linux 2.4	Solaris	Other UNIX	Windows
Event	linux-sysepoll	linux-rtsig	solaris-devpoll	Poll	Give up all
Network	sendfile64	sendfile	sendfilev	sendfile	hope

    Use `sendfile64` only if large files (>2GB) are disabled, which we should do if we do not serve files that big.

2. If we have dynamic content, we should choose our CGI protocol wisely. FastCGI and SCGI are better choices than CGI. If you have the luxury of choosing your CGI language, you might want to try a small and fast scripting language such as Python or even Lua.

3. Static data is best served from static files. The usual file systems in use today will easily outperform any database/CGI solution. If we have a big page with lots of JavaScript and a smaller part of the page is dynamic (for example, not the JavaScript), we should put the JavaScript in a static `.js` file and link them.

4. Use SSL only for sensitive data. Clients do not cache data sent over SSL. So if we have images or other static data that does not compromise the client's information, send it over to plain HTTP.

5. Remove unused modules from the configuration. This is a win-win option for both speed and memory.

There are some settings that affect speed and stability, and depend on the scenario we deploy Lighttpd in. For example, if we have a huge number of concurrent connections open, we can run out of file descriptors. We can counter that by increasing the number of file descriptors in the kernel and setting `server.max-fds` higher (default is 1024). If we have a lot of small requests, we might increase `server.max-keepalive-requests`. On the other hand, if we send out a few big files at any given time, we might want to increase the send buffer (note that this has to be allocated for each request, so it might eat into our memory pretty fast). The following are the three scenarios with settings that should give good performance:

1. **Many small requests** (typical for AJAX applications): The defaults are quite good here, although for big applications we might raise `server.max-keep-alive-requests` to 256 or even higher (try how many sessions we can keep alive without running into the file handle barrier).

2. **Big requests** (for example, YouTube): Increase the send file buffer; for example, on Linux set the kernel configuration to:
   ```
   net.ipv4.tcp_wmem = 4096 65536 524288
   net.core.wmem_max = 1048576
   ```
   On BSD set `net.inet.tcp.sendspace = 8192` (or even higher, but remember it eats a lot of the kernel RAM per open connection).

3. **Big files upload** (for whatever): Do the same to the read file buffer: Under Linux do the same as in step 3, but replace "wmem" with "rmem", and under BSD set `net.inet.tcp.recvspace = 8192`.

With any server that handles many requests per second, a huge pile of file descriptors is a good thing to have. Note that other applications are also using up file descriptors, for example, the CGI backends (if we have more than one).

These are just common scenarios and some tips to work with them. In any case, run `http_load` and look at the result. If the throughput is higher, and/or the latency lower, good! If not, roll back the change and try something else.

Specific Optimizations

Until now, our methods and tools to measure performance are quite blunt—we can see how fast our Lighttpd is with a specific optimization, but we do not know where to start. **Ahmdahl's law** (see `http://en.wikipedia.org/wiki/Amdahl%27s_law`) implies that *if we optimize a portion of the code that takes up a portion X of the time by the ratio Y, the resulting speedup is limited by X*. The downside of this is optimizing code that never gets called which is a good way to throw away our time. The upside is that if we know which portions of the code takes up most of the time, we know where to optimize.

A crude way of finding out where Lighttpd spends its time (at least between reading and writing) is log timing. As of Lighttpd 1.5.0, there is a new configuration option: `debug.log-timing`. This option can be enabled to insert timing information into the log files. For each request, the start time plus three intervals will be timed. The interval between receiving and queuing the request, the time used for reading the request, and the time used for writing a response, is in the following format:

```
write-start: #.#### read-queue-wait: #### ms read-time: #### ms
write-time: #### ms
```

This timing can be helpful if we want to know whether we should spend our time on optimizing the read cycle or the write cycle. As a rule of thumb, if we have a big `read-queue-wait` time, we may have too many requests. So increasing file handles or maybe even load-balancing on multiple systems might help. If there is a long read time, look out for uploads or big forms, and try to select a better event handler. If the write time is long see if we can improve the network backend; or if Lighttpd serves a dynamic page, see if we can improve the web application. Perhaps we can use a different CGI backend, introduce caching, and use `mod_magnet` for very small tasks.

Example: Caching with mod_magnet

Suppose we have a PHP script that runs through a database, fetches a set of records, and creates a HTML page. So far so slow; our database, PHP interpreter, and CGI interface are taxed on every request. Further, suppose that we do not really need millisecond up-to-date data. We could run the PHP script say every five minutes, thus improving its performance as it runs.

Firstly, we can change our PHP script to write the HTML output into a file instead of standard output and send a `X-Lighttpd-Sendfile` header (enable this in the CGI backend configuration—refer to Appendix B). This has two benefits: Lighttpd can send out the file directly with no speed penalty and we have the cached file. Make sure our Lighttpd is built with Lua support. Now, we can add the following configuration:

```
server.modules = ( ..., "mod_magnet", ...)
magnet.attract-physical-path-to = ("/application/" => "app.lua")
```

Our `app.lua` can then use the cache to see if the file is older than five minutes and if so call the PHP. The following code does exactly that:

```
-- app.lua: cache a PHP application for 5 minutes
php_path = "/app.php"
cache_dir = lighty.env["physical.doc-root"] .. "/cache/"
cache_time = 300 -- 300 seconds = 5 minutes

path = lighty.env["physical.rel-path"]
```

```
s = lighty.stat(cache_dir .. path)
if s ~= nil then -- not in cache, call out to PHP
  lighty.env["request.uri"] = php_path
  return lighty.RESTART_REQUEST
end
if s[8] + cache_time > os.time() then -- too old, call out to PHP
  lighty.env["request.uri"] = php_path
  return lighty.RESTART_REQUEST
end
lighty.header["Content-Type"] = "text/html"
lighty.content = {{ filename = cache_dir .. path }}
return 200
```

This may look like a special case, but there are many web applications out there which do not use any caching at the application level. Plus, its integration into the web server makes this a winning performance for all cases. When the page is cached, it is served almost as fast as a static file.

On the other hand, if the page is not in the cache or is too old, the X-Lighttpd-Sendfile header trick at least reduces the number of file handles needed for the transaction and improves the throughput by shifting the work from our Lighttpd process to the operating system.

Measuring System Load

From a holistic viewpoint (or if we plan to invest in hardware), we might be interested in the resource, which is limiting the performance of our Lighttpd. Most UNIX-like systems have a command, vmstat, which shows a small table of system load parameters:

procs		---------memory----------			--swap--		---io---		--system-		----cpu----			
r	b	swpd	free	buff	cache	si	so	bi	bo	in	cs	us	sy	id	wa
1	0	0	302064	0	0	0	0	0	0	0	0	0	0	100	0

In this case, the system is sitting idle. The following fields are of particular interest:

Section / Field	Description
memory / swpd	The amount of swap space used. Ideally, it should be zero. If our Lighttpd gets swapped out, the performance will degrade dramatically.
memory / free	The amount of free memory. If this gets close to zero, watch out for swapping.
io / bi io / bo	The amount of blocks received and sent, respectively. Nothing bad to see here.
cpu / us cpu / sy	The user mode and kernel mode CPU times, as percentage of available CPU time. Add them. If it is close to 100, we need more CPU capacity.
cpu / id	The percentage of time the CPU sits idle. If greater than zero, our CPU load is quite healthy.
cpu / wa	This is the percentage of time the CPU had to wait for IO. This is of special interest to us, as it shows whether we are in need of more threads, a different IO backend, and so on.

Under Microsoft Windows operating systems, the task manager shows CPU load, memory/swap file usage, and network performance. If one of these maxes out, we have a candidate for improvement. The basic idea is the same as with the UNIX-like systems.

Profiling with gprof

To see where Lighttpd is spending its time in more detail, the use of a profiler is recommended. gcc comes with a profiling tool called gprof. We first need to tell gcc to prepare a Lighttpd version for profiling, then put it under load with http_load, stop Lighttpd, and run gprof to get a list of functions sorted by the time spent, which we can then interpret to see what to optimize. Now, let's see each step in more detail.

We can create a gprof ready Lighttpd by specifying a flag for the C compiler. This is done with the following commands before calling configure:

```
$ export CFLAGS=-pg
$ export LDFLAGS=-pg
```

Otherwise, proceed as in Chapter 1 to create a Lighttpd build. We might also want to install this Lighttpd in a location different from our production build, as the profiling code will slow down our Lighttpd just slightly, and may also fill our file system with profiling data while running. So use the `configure -prefix` argument to specify a different location, for example, `configure -prefix=/opt/lighttpd-gprof`.

The build might fail with an error of "undefined references to _mcount"

In this case, edit the `libtool` shell script created by `configure`. Search for a line `compiler_flags=` and add `-pg` so that the line says `compiler_flags=-pg`. Now `make clean all` should build our Lighttpd with profiling support.

Given that our build succeeded, we can now execute our profiling Lighttpd and test load to get the profiling data.

Load Testing our Profiling Build

Our profiling build can be run exactly as usual. For directions on load testing using `http_load`, see the example. For this example, we use a 100-byte HTML file and set `http_load` to fetch 10,000 times with 10 parallel connections. After running the test and stopping our Lighttpd, we should find a new file with the name `gmon.out` (given a post-20th century-version of `gprof`). We can now run `gprof` to get some statistics. `gprof` needs at least two parameters: the path to the Lighttpd executable and the path to the `gmon.out`, our profiling run just created. For example:

```
$ gprof /opt/lighttpd-gprof/sbin/lighttpd gmon.out
```

This will show a lot of text, including two interesting tables: the **flat profile** and the **call graph**. The flat profile is a table of functions with a percentage of the full runtime, the cumulative runtime in seconds, the internal runtime (self) in seconds, the number of calls, the internal and cumulative runtimes per call, and finally the function name.

The **cumulative runtime** of a function is the time from when the first line of the function is executed until the execution returns from the function, whereas the **internal runtime** is the complete runtime minus the sum of complete runtimes of all functions called from the function.

The flat profile is very helpful to determine where our time is best spent optimizing. For us, the internal runtime and the number of calls show how much an optimization might affect total performance. The list is ordered by the percentage of the total time. So the higher on the list a function is, the more time we can shave off by optimizing it. The following is our example flat profile:

% time	cumulative seconds	self seconds	calls	self ms/call	total ms/call	name
12.79	0.50	0.50	10000	0.05	0.08	http_request_parse
7.42	0.79	0.29	150179	0.00	0.00	array_get_index
5.63	1.01	0.22	370497	0.00	0.00	buffer_caseless...
4.35	1.18	0.17	13806	0.01	0.02	connection_hand...
3.84	1.33	0.15	20128	0.01	0.02	connection_reset
3.84	1.48	0.15	20599	0.01	0.16	connection_stat...
3.32	1.61	0.13	300039	0.00	0.00	buffer_append_s...
3.07	1.73	0.12	10000	0.01	0.06	http_response_p...
2.56	1.83	0.10	10000	0.01	0.05	http_response_w...
2.56	1.93	0.10	10000	0.01	0.01	network_write_c...
2.30	2.02	0.09	370095	0.00	0.00	buffer_prepare_...
2.30	2.11	0.09	40018	0.00	0.00	LI_ltostr
1.66	2.18	0.07	350705	0.00	0.00	buffer_prepare_...
1.66	2.24	0.07	120001	0.00	0.00	buffer_is_equal
1.66	2.31	0.07	633052	0.00	0.00	buffer_reset
1.53	2.37	0.06	310064	0.00	0.00	buffer_copy_str...
1.53	2.43	0.06	80855	0.00	0.00	chunkqueue_remo...
1.53	2.49	0.06	10000	0.01	0.01	connection_close
1.53	2.55	0.06				__divdi3
1.53	2.61	0.06	70019	0.00	0.00	array_insert_un...
1.28	2.66	0.05	120000	0.00	0.00	buffer_append_s...
1.28	2.71	0.05	20000	0.00	0.00	hashme
1.28	2.76	0.05	10000	0.01	0.02	stat_cache_get_...
1.28	2.81	0.05				etag_mutate
1.02	2.85	0.04	60384	0.00	0.00	array_reset
1.02	2.89	0.04	40018	0.00	0.00	buffer_append_long
1.02	2.93	0.04	30256	0.00	0.00	config_setup_co...
1.02	2.97	0.04	10238	0.00	0.02	connection_accept
1.02	3.01	0.04	10000	0.00	0.02	network_write_c...
1.02	3.05	0.04	10000	0.00	0.01	request_check_h...
...	...	...	...	...	...	...

The long function names were cut off in the name of readability, as well as all the following functions one percent of the runtime. As we can see, the `http_request_parse` function takes the biggest chunk of runtime. This should be so, given that we are sending out the same short file over and over again, which should be cached from the second request onwards. Note that the `http_request_parse` function would be top priority on our list should we want to optimize the code, because it has the biggest internal runtime and also gets a decent number of calls (one per request).

An even more detailed report is the call graph. It shows a table for every function with a list of callers before and a list of callees after it. For each entry, the time (complete and internal), and the number of calls (from the parent function and total) is shown. We can use this to find out why a function is called so often, and trace the code paths. However, without a decent visualization, we can easily get lost in the mountains of data. Here is an example call tree (again, function names are cut off for brevity):

```
index   % time  self   children   called        name
                                                 <spontaneous>
[1]      94.7   0.01   3.69                      main [1]
                0.00   1.90       288/288        network_server_h... [3]
                0.08   1.67       10599/20599    connection_state... [2]
                0.00   0.02       1/1            connections_free [60]
                0.01   0.01       599/599        connection_hand... [61]
                0.00   0.00       1/1            config_read [90]
                0.00   0.00       1/1            server_free [95]
                0.00   0.00       2/3            log_error_write [104]
                0.00   0.00       1/1            plugins_load [107]
                0.00   0.00       4/50159        array_get_element [15]
                0.00   0.00       1/1            log_error_open [109]
                0.00   0.00       1/1            network_init [110]
                0.00   0.00       292/292        stat_cache_tri... [111]
                0.00   0.00       1/1            plugins_free [115]
                0.00   0.00       1/1            config_set_def... [117]
                0.00   0.00       1/1            server_init [122]
                0.00   0.00       1/10001        fdevent_unregister [42]
                0.00   0.00       1/1            network_close [124]
                0.00   0.00       1/1            network_regist... [127]
                0.00   0.00       1/26794        fdevent_event_del [64]
                0.00   0.00       10599/20599    plugins_call_h... [133]
```

index	% time	self	children	called	name
		0.00	0.00	887/887	fdevent_event_... [150]
		0.00	0.00	887/887	fdevent_event_... [149]
		0.00	0.00	887/887	fdevent_event_... [148]
		0.00	0.00	887/887	fdevent_get_ha... [152]
		0.00	0.00	887/887	fdevent_get_co... [151]
		0.00	0.00	639/639	fdevent_poll [156]
		0.00	0.00	292/292	plugins_call_h... [160]
		0.00	0.00	1/1	plugins_call_init [188]
		0.00	0.00	1/1	plugins_call_s... [189]
		0.00	0.00	1/1	fdevent_init [180]
		0.00	0.00	1/1	stat_cache_init [192]
		0.00	0.00	1/10001	fdevent_fcntl_set [134]
		0.00	0.00	1/1	log_error_close [186]
---	---	---	---	---	---
		0.07	1.58	10000/20599	network_server_h... [3]
		0.08	1.67	10599/20599	main [1]
[2]	86.9	0.15	3.25	20599	connection_state_mac... [2]
		0.02	1.07	10000/10000	connection_handl... [4]
		0.50	0.28	10000/10000	http_request_parse [5]
		0.12	0.50	10000/10000	http_response_pr... [6]
		0.16	0.06	13207/13806	connection_hand... [14]
		0.02	0.18	10000/10000	connection_hand... [19]
		0.07	0.10	10000/20128	connection_reset [10]
...	...	...	...	...	...

Although we now have specific numbers where our Lighttpd uses its time, and even which functions gets called from where, we still do not know how to optimize the settings to reduce the runtime.

Alas, unless we want to optimize directly in the source code (which thanks to Lighttpd underlying the revised BSD license and being available in source form, we can), there is no easy way apart from trial and error to find out which setting creates which effect. At least, we can see where this effect comes into play.

Summary

Knowing *what* to optimize beats knowing *how* to optimize. Therefore, load testing and collecting usage statistics (see last chapter) is paramount to improving throughput and minimizing latency. Probably, the most important thing about optimization is to know when to stop.

At the moment, there is no easier way than trial and error to find out what makes our Lighttpd work faster. On the other hand, optimizing for performance may conflict with other goals such as security and maintainability.

Logging the timing of the request or response phases can give us a broad overview where to optimize first. Knowing which system resources limit our Lighttpd's performance can also give us a hint on what to do. If we need a more detailed picture of where our Lighttpd spends its time, profiling is our course of action.

10
Migration from Apache

The most common web server used today is still Apache, so whilst we wait for Lighttpd world domination, the migration from this server warrants its own chapter. As this is a book on Lighttpd and not on Apache, this chapter assumes some knowledge of the Apache configuration. If anything is unclear, the Apache documentation at `http://apache.org/docs/` will hopefully help.

Now starting from a working Apache installation, what can Lighttpd offer us?

- Improved performance for most cases (as in more hits per second)
- Reduced CPU time and memory usage
- Improved security (refer to Chapter 8 to maximize your return on investment)

Of course, the move to Lighttpd is not a small one, especially if our Apache configuration makes use of its many features. Systems tied into Apache as a module may make the move hard or even impossible without porting the module to a Lighttpd module or moving the functionality into CGI programs, if possible.

We can ease the pain by moving in small steps. The following descriptions assume that we have one Apache instance running on one hardware instance. But we can scale the method by repeating it for every hardware instance.

When not to migrate

Before we start this journey, we need to know that our hardware and operating systems support Lighttpd, that we have root access (or access to someone who has), and that the system has enough space for another Lighttpd installation (yes, I know, Lighttpd should *reduce* space concerns, but I have seen Apache installations munching away entire RAID arrays). Probably, this only makes sense if we plan on moving a big percentage of traffic to Lighttpd. We also might make extensive use of Apache module, which means a complete migration would involve finding or writing suitable substitutes for Lighttpd.

Adding Lighttpd to the Mix

Install Lighttpd on the system that Apache runs on. Refer to Chapter 1 for installation instructions. Find an unused port (refer to a port scanner if needed) to set `server.port` to. For example, if port 4080 is unused on our system, we would look for `server.port` in our Lighttpd configuration and change it to:

```
server.port = 4080
```

If we want to use SSL, we should change all occurrences of the port 443 to another free port, say 4443. We assume our Apache is answering requests on HTTP port 80.

Now let's use this Lighttpd instance as a proxy for our Apache by adding the following configuration:

```
server.modules = (
  #...
  "mod_proxy",
  #...
)

#...

proxy.server = (
  "" => { # proxy everything
    host => "127.0.0.1" # localhost
    port => "80"
  )
)
```

This tells our Lighttpd to proxy all requests to the server that answers on localhost, port 80, which happens to be our Apache server. Now, when we start our Lighttpd and point our browser to `http://localhost:4080/`, we should be able to see the same thing our Apache is returning.

What is a proxy?

A **Proxy** stands in front of another object, simulating the proxied object by relaying all requests to it. A proxy can change requests on the fly, filter requests, and so on. In our case, Lighttpd is the web server to the outside, whilst Apache will still get all requests as usual.

Excursion: mod_proxy

mod_proxy is the module that allows Lighttpd to relay requests to another web server. It is not to be confused with mod_proxy_core (of Lighttpd 1.5.0), which provides a basis for other interfaces such as CGI. Usually, we want to proxy only a specific subset of requests, for example, we might want to proxy requests for Java server pages to a Tomcat server. This could be done with the following proxy directive:

```
proxy.server = (
   ".jsp" => ( host => "127.0.0.1", port => "8080" )
                            # given our tomcat is on port 8080
)
```

Thus the tomcat server only serves JSPs, which is what it was built to do, whilst our Lighttpd does the rest.

Or we might have another server which we want to include in our Web presence at some given directory:

```
proxy.server = (
   "/somepath" => ( host => "127.0.0.1", port => "8080" )
)
```

Assuming the server is on port 8080, this will do the trick. Now http://localhost/somepath/index.html will be the same as http://localhost:8080/index.html.

Reducing Apache Load

Note that as most Lighttpd directives, proxy.server can be moved into a selector (refer to Chapter 2), thereby reducing its reach. This way, we can reduce the set of files Apache will have to touch in a phased manner. For example, YouTube™ uses Lighttpd to serve the videos. Usually, we want to make Lighttpd serve static files such as images, CSS, and JavaScript, leaving Apache to serve the dynamically generated pages.

Now, we have two options: we can either filter the extensions we want Apache to handle, or we can filter the addresses we want Lighttpd to serve without asking Apache.

Actually, the first can be done in two ways. Assuming we want to give all addresses ending with `.cgi` and `.php` to Apache, we could either use the matching of `proxy.server`:

```
proxy.server = (
    ".cgi" => ( host = "127.0.0.1", port = "8080" ),
    ".php" => ( host = "127.0.0.1", port = "8080" )
)
```

or match by selector:

```
$HTTP['url'] =~ "(.cgi|.php)$" {
    proxy.server = ( "" => ( host = "127.0.0.1", port = "8080" ) )
}
```

The second way also allows negative filtering and filtering by `regexp`—just use `!~` instead of `=~`.

mod_perl, mod_php, and mod_python

There are no Lighttpd modules to embed scripting languages into Lighttpd (with the exception of `mod_magnet`, which embeds Lua) because this is simply not the Lighttpd way of doing things. Instead, we have the CGI, SCGI, and FastCGI interfaces (refer to Chapter 7) to outsource this work to the respective interpreters. In the next chapter, there will be sample installations and configurations for some popular applications.

Most `mod_perl` scripts are easily converted to FastCGI using `CGI::Fast`. Usually, our `mod_perl` script will look a lot like the following script:

```
use CGI;
my $q = CGI->new;
initialize(); # this might need to be done only once
process_query($q); # this should be done per request
print response($q); # this, too
```

Using the easiest way to convert to FastCGI:

```
use CGI:Fast # instead of CGI
while (my $q = CGI:Fast->new) { # get requests in a while-loop
    initialize();
    process_query($q);
    print response($q);
}
```

If this runs, we may try to put the `initialize()` call outside of the loop to make our script run even faster than under `mod_perl`. However, this is just the basic case. There are `mod_perl` scripts that manipulate the Apache core or use special hooks, so these scripts can get a little more complicated to migrate.

Migrating from `mod_php` to `php-fcgi` is easier—we do not need to change the scripts, just the configuration. This means that we do not get the benefits of an obvious request loop, but we can work around that by setting some global variables only if they are not already set. The security benefit is obvious. Even for Apache, there are some alternatives to `mod_php`, which try to provide more security, often with bad performance implications.

`mod_python` can be a little more complicated, because Apache calls out to the python functions directly, converting form fields to function arguments on the fly. If we are lucky, our python scripts could implement the **WSGI (Web Server Gateway Interface)**. In this case, we can just use a WSGI-FastCGI wrapper. Looking on the Web, I already found two: one standalone (`http://svn.saddi.com/py-lib/trunk/fcgi.py`), and one, a part of the PEAK project (`http://peak.telecommunity.com/DevCenter/FrontPage`). Otherwise, python usually has excellent support for SCGI.

As with `mod_perl`, there are some internals that have to be moved into the configuration (for example dynamic 404 pages, the directive for this is `server.error-handler-405`, which can also point to a CGI script). However, for basic scripts, we can use SCGI (either from `http://www.mems-exchange.org/software/scgi/` or as a python-only version from `http://www.cherokee-project.com/download/pyscgi/`). We also need to change `import cgi` to `import scgi` and change `CGIHandler` and `CGIServer` to `SCGIHandler` and `SCGIServer`, respectively.

.htaccess

A lot of Lighttpd users converting from Apache ask if Lighttpd has any substitutes for `.htaccess` files, which were made popular by Apache and are now a de-facto Standard used by many web servers. Instead, Lighttpd has its own configuration syntax, so all the old `.htaccess` files won't work with Lighttpd.

There is no perfect solution to this problem, but as the most used feature of `.htaccess` files is authentication, we can at least solve that. Let's have a look at the authentication directive format in Apache and Lighttpd:

- Apache just assumes that the path required for authentication is the path where the `.htaccess` file resides, while Lighttpd needs to add this explicitly.

- The `httpd.conf` adds some more stuff, which is given as default from `httpd.conf`. In the `lighttpd.conf` example, we do not assume such defaults.

Note that the Lighttpd configuration gets a little more complicated if we have multiple backends or user files. In this case, we need to use a selector to limit the reach of our directives. For example, assume that we want digest authentication for internal.mydomain.com, but htpasswd authentication for some directories in mydomain.com, with a different htpasswd file for the messages directory:

```
server.modules = (..., "mod_auth", ...)

auth.backend = "htpasswd"
auth.backend.htpasswd.userfile = "/web/general/.htpasswd"

$HTTP["host"] == "internal.mydomain.com" {
  auth.backend = "htdigest"
  auth.backend.htdigest.userfile = "/web/internal/.htdigest"
  auth.require = (
    "/" => (
      "method" => "digest",
      "realm" => "internal",
      "require" => "valid-user"
    )
  )
}
else
$HTTP["url"] =~ "^/messages" {
  auth.backend.htpasswd.userfile = "/web/messages/.htpasswd"
  auth.require = (
    "/" => (
      "method" => "basic",
      "realm" => "messages",
      "require" => "valid-user"
    )
  )
}

auth.require = ( # This table assigns authentication requirements
                # to directories or file types.
  "/admin/" => ( # everything below the /admin path
    "method" => "basic",
    "realm" => "admin",
    "require" => "user=andre|user=bob" # allow only bob and me
  ),
  "/download" => (
    "method" => "basic",
    "realm" => "download",
    "require" => "valid-user"
  ),
```

```
  ".private" => ( # all files ending with .private
    "method" => "basic",
    "realm" => "private",
    "require" => "user=andre"
  )
  # ... we could add more directories here.
)
```

The first selector marks out a region `internal.mydomain.com`, where we then use digest authentication. The next selector catches the message directory everywhere else and includes the use of the `/web/messages/.htpasswd` user file. Finally, we add all the requirements for the other directories.

Note that the following two are identical:

```
$HTTP["url"] =~ "^/messages" {
auth.require = ( "/" => ( ... ) )          auth.require = ( "/messages" => ( ... ) )
}
```

But the left version is more flexible as it allows defining different user files and backends for each path that matches a certain pattern. Armed with this knowledge, we can write a small script that runs through our web root, finds all `.htaccess` files and emits corresponding Lighttpd configuration (at least for the access directives). In fact we do not even need to do this, because I already did the coding:

```
#!/bin/env python
import os
def toUserList(users):
  return "|".join(["user="+user for user in users.split(" ")])
  def groups(groupFileName, gps):
  groupFile = open(groupFileName)
  groupDict = {}
  for groupLine in groupFile:group, users = groupLine.split(":")
      groupDict[group.strip()] = users.strip()
      return "|".join([toUserList(groupDict[g])
                       for g in gps.split(" ")])
for (root, dirs, files) in os.walk(path):
  if ".htaccess" not in files: continue
  filepath = os.path.join(root, ".htaccess")
  f = open(filepath)
  try:
    realm = root.rsplit(os.path.sep, 1)[1]
  except:
    realm = root
  try:
```

```
          # try some sensible defaults
          r = {"authtype":"Basic", "url":root,
              "required":"nothing","realm":realm,
              "authuserfile":os.path.join(root, ".htpasswd",
              "error":None}
          for line in f:
            try:
              tempdirective, arguments = line.split(" ", 1)
              directive = tempdirective.lower()
                r[directive] = arguments.strip('"')
            except:
              pass
            if r["required"].startswith("user"):
              r["required"] = toUserList(r["required"][5:])
            elif r["required"].startswith("group"):
              r["required"] = groups(r["authgroupfile"], r["required"][6:])
            if r["required"] != "nothing" and r["error"] is None:
              r["backend"] = {"Basic":"htpasswd",
                    "Digest":"htdigest"}[r["authtype"]]
            r["authtype"] = r["authtype"].lower()
            print """$HTTP["url"] =~ "%{url}s" {
      auth.backend = "${backend}s"
      auth.backend.${backend}s.userfile = "${authuserfile}s"
      auth.require = ( "/" => (
        "method" => "${authtype}s",
        "realm" => "${realm}s",
        "require" => "${required}s"
      ) )
    }""" % r;
      finally:
        f.close()
```

The `htaccess2lighttpd.py` script is available at
`http://www.packtpub.com/files/code/2103_Code.zip`.

Note the script does have one limitation: Lighttpd does not handle groups. However, it allows specification of a list of users directly, as in `user=andre|user=bob` that we required for admin access. The other way is to have a separate password file for each group. The script, however, takes the first way. This means that we need to re-run the script each time a group membership changes. So this solution would only be temporary — the move to per-group access files can then be made without being hectic.

.htaccess and PHP

Apart from that, some users might put PHP options into the `.htaccess` files. **Pier Alan Joye** maintains a `htscanner` program to ease the transition. It is available at `http://pecl.php.net/package/htscanner`. This program basically moves PHP options from `.htaccess` files into the `php.ini` file.

Rewriting Rules

On the Lighttpd forums, most former Apache administrators ask how they can adapt their rewrite rules to work with Lighttpd. There is no program (yet) to do this, but here are some typical constructs and advice on how to do that in Lighttpd lingua:

Apache	Lighttpd
LoadModule "rewrite_module" RewriteEngine on	server.modules = (..., "mod_rewrite", "mod_redirect", ...)

# A simple rewrite 	
RewriteRule ^from_here(.*)/to_there$1
	# refer to Chapter 2
	url.rewrite = ("^/from_here" => "to_there")

RewriteCond %{HTTP_HOST} me\..*
RewriteRule ^/(.*) /me/$1
	$HTTP["host"] =~ "me\..*" {
	    url.rewrite = ("^/" => "/me/"
	}

# Redirecting a single file RewriteRule move.html target.html [R]	url.redirect = ("move.html" => "target.html")
# Solving the trailing slash problem RewriteCond %{REQUEST_FILENAME} -d RewriteRule (.*) $1/	# nothing to do here. Lighttpd does not # have this problem.
# Redirecting failed web pages to xyz.com RewriteCond %{REQUEST_FILENAME} !-f RewriteRule ^(.+) http://xyz.com/$1	# use an CGI error page that redirects server-error-handler-404 = "redirect.cgi" # see Chapter 12 on how to do this in lua
# Time-based multiplexing RewriteCond %{TIME_HOUR} > 07 RewriteCond %{TIME_HOUR} < 19 RewriteRule ^foo.html foo.day.html RewriteRule ^foo.html foo.night.html	# either use mod_magnet, see Chapter 12, or solve this outside of Lighttpd, for example by using a cron job to set symbolic links.

Apache	Lighttpd

# Rewrite for google bot 	
RewriteCond %{HTTP_USER_AGENT} \
   Google
RewriteRule ^(.+) /bots/$1
	# match for useragent
	$HTTP["useragent"] =~ "Google" {
	    url.rewrite = "^/" => "/bots"
	}

# Rewrite by cookie (missing session) 	
RewriteCond %{HTTP_COOKIE} sess [N]
RewriteRule ^(.+) index.php
	# use a negative regexp match
	$HTTP["cookie"] !~ "sess" {
	    url.rewrite = ("(.*)" => "index.pho")
	}

# set environment variable based on query 	
RewriteCond %{QUERY_STRING} \
   id=([^&]*)
RewriteRule ^(.*)$ /$1 [E=ID:%1]
	server.modules += ("mod_setenv")
	$HTTP["url"] =~ "[?&]id=([^&]*)" {
	    setenv.add_request_header = "ID: %1"
	}

# block images by referer 	
RewriteCond %{REFERER} !^$
RewriteCond %{REFERER} !my\.net [NC]
RewriteRule ^images/*.png - [F]
	# deny for non-empty outside referers
	$HTTP["referer"] !~ "^($|.*my\.net) {
	    url.access-deny = (".png")
	}

Naturally this table cannot cover all aspects of Apache rewrite rules, but remember that all complex systems have emerged from simple systems. The following chapter will show how to set up some oft-used web applications with Lighttpd.

WebDAV

Apache does WebDAV out of the box, while Lighttpd needs the mod_webdav module to support WebDAV, and it still has some rough edges. For example, Window users will find that their mod_auth login does not work when they activate WebDAV; this can be compensated by a cookie-based login. Oh, and we need to have webdav support configured at compile time, if we built our Lighttpd from source. The configuration, as always, is pretty straightforward:

```
server.modules += ( "mod_webdav" )

# activate WebDAV for the server "dav.my.net"
$HTTP["host"] == "dav.my.net" {
webdav.activate = "enable"
```

```
# enable writing for members only (identify by sess cookie)
$HTTP["cookie"] !~ "sess" {
  $HTTP["url"] =~ "^/members/" {
    webdav.is-readonly = "enable"
  }
}
}
```

The important directives here are `webdav.activate` and `webdav.is-readonly`. The former activates WebDAV, if we set it to `enable`. Otherwise, WebDAV is deactivated by default. The latter forbids operations that modify files on the server (PUT and DELETE), and is disabled by default. So unless we enable this option, PUT and DELETES are served.

Summary

There are some obstacles on the way from Apache to Lighttpd. But a planned and careful approach will allow us to keep our server working while we change it. The `.htaccess` scanner script can be a stop gap measure to smoothen the transition for `.htaccess` authentication users. Finally, a heavy use of rewrite rules can make it tricky to move. However, we can translate them one by one into something that will work with Lighttpd, especially when we add Lua to the mix as we will show in the following chapter.

11
CGI Revisited

In this chapter, we will go through some example setups of popular web applications and frameworks, and see how they can be made to work with Lighttpd. We will set up the following popular applications and frameworks:

- Ruby on Rails
- WordPress
- PhPMyAdmin
- MediaWiki
- trac
- AWStats
- AjaxTerm

Now without further ado, let's configure our Lighttpd to work with Rails:

Ruby on Rails

Ruby on Rails is a popular web application framework that has generated a lot of hype since 2006. We can find it at `http://www.rubyonrails.org`. It usually works with Apache, but with some simple configuration and `mod_fastcgi` we can make it fly with Lighttpd.

Ensure a full FastCGI installation

As stated in Chapter 1, depending on our system, we might need to add fastcgi-devel packages to actually use it. If our Lighttpd has `mod_fastcgi`, we should be fine.

First, if we do not already have `mod_fastcgi`, we need to install the Ruby interpreter. The download page at `http://www.ruby-lang.org/de/downloads/` has directions for Ubuntu Linux and Mac OS X, as well as an installer for Windows. The installation should be quite simple. Just follow the instructions on the page.

Next, we need RubyGems, the ruby package install manager. This is also a simple download and installation (using Ruby itself). Download this from `http://rubyforge.org/frs/download.php/38646/rubygems-1.2.0.tgz`, unpack the distribution, and install it with the following command:

```
$ ruby setup.rb
mkdir -p /usr/local/lib/ruby/site_ruby/1.8
mkdir -p /usr/local/bin
mkdir -p /usr/local/lib/ruby/site_ruby/1.8/rbconfig
install -c -m 0644 rbconfig/datadir.rb /usr/local/lib/ruby/site_ruby/1.8/
rbconfig/datadir.rb
mkdir -p /usr/local/lib/ruby/site_ruby/1.8/rubygems
install -c -m 0644 rubygems/builder.rb /usr/local/lib/ruby/site_ruby/1.8/
rubygems/builder.rb
... [lots of text omitted] ...
RubyGems installed the following executables:

        /usr/local/bin/gem
```

If gem was installed by a previous RubyGems installation, you may need to remove it manually.

With RubyGems installed, we can use it to automatically download and install Rails with the following command:

```
$ gem install rails
Successfully installed rake-0.8.1
Successfully installed activesupport-2.1.0
Successfully installed activerecord-2.1.0
Successfully installed actionpack-2.1.0
Successfully installed actionmailer-2.1.0
Successfully installed activeresource-2.1.0
Successfully installed rails-2.1.0
7 gems installed
Installing ri documentation for rake-0.8.1...
... [ Installing ri documentation for all other packages ] ...
Installing ri documentation for activeresource-2.1.0...
```

```
Installing RDoc documentation for rake-0.8.1...
... [ Installing RDoc documentation for all other packages ] ...
Installing RDoc documentation for activeresource-2.1.0...
```

Now for the sake of this example, let's presume that we create a rails application at /web/railsapp, which would be initiated with the following command:

```
$ rails /web/railsapp
      create
      create   app/controllers
      create   app/helpers
      create   app/models
      create   app/views/layouts
      create   config/environments
      create   config/initializers
      create   db
      create   doc
... [ creating lots of other stuff ] ...
      create   doc/README_FOR_APP
      create   log/server.log
      create   log/production.log
      create   log/development.log
      create   log/test.log
```

Finally, we add our rails application to Lighttpd. To do this, we need to make sure we have the necessary modules:

```
server.modules += ("mod_rewrite", "mod_redirect", "mod_fastcgi")
```

We may want our Lighttpd to serve only this Rails application. In this case, we just need to set the document-root to our Rails application's public directory:

```
server.document-root = "/web/railsapp/public"
```

Alternatively, we could want to have a subdomain or a subdirectory where our Rails application will reside.

Either:

```
$HTTP["host"] == "rails.ourdomain.com" {
  server.document-root = "/web/railsapp/public"
}
```

or:

```
$HTTP["url"] =~ "/rails/" {
   server.document-root = "/web/railsapp/public"
   url.rewrite = ("/rails" => "")
}
```

If we use Lighttpd 1.4, we can tell it to start the rails application for us and also to **respawn** them (this is what computer science folks call restarting a process which has died — poetic, isn't it?) should they die:

```
fastcgi.server = (
   ".fcgi" => (
      (
         "min-procs" => 1,
         "max-procs" => 5,
         "socket" => "/tmp/rails_fcgi.socket",
         "bin-path" => "/www/railsapp/public/dispatch.fastcgi",
         "docroot" => "/www/railsapp/public"
      )
   )
)
```

For Lighttpd since 1.5.0, we need the `spawn-fcgi` script, which is included with the Lighttpd package. We can run it as follows:

```
spawn-fcgi -f /www/railsapp/public/dispatch.fastcgi -s \
   /tmp/rails-fcgi.socket -C 5
```

Then we can use the code as above but for the `bin-path` setting, which is no longer required.

We also want to make sure that HTML files and `fcgi` files are served automatically if they are present, and that `dispatch.fcgi` is invoked otherwise:

```
server.index-files = ("index.html", "index.fcgi")
server.error-handler-404 = "/dispatch.fcgi"
```

Now let's pull those pieces together:

```
server.modules = ( ..., "mod_fastcgi", ...)

$HTTP["host"] == "rails.ourdomain.com" {
   server.index-files = ("index.html", "index.fcgi")
   server.error-handler-404 = "/dispatch.fcgi"
   server.document-root = "/web/railsapp/public"
   fastcgi.server = (
```

```
".fcgi" => (
  (
  "min-procs" => 1,
  "max-procs" => 5,
  "socket" => "/tmp/rails_fcgi.socket",
  # alternatively use spawn-fcgi as above
  "bin-path" => "/www/railsapp/public/dispatch.fcgi",
  "docroot" => "/www/railsapp/public"
  )
  )
  )
}
```

Voilà! Our rails application is now served by Lighttpd! By the way, FastCGI is not the only alternative. Zed Shaw has also created a Rails application for the SCGI connector. Install it with the following command line (at the time of this writing, the latest version available was 0.4.3; change it appropriately):

```
$ wget http://www.zedshaw.com/downloads/scgi_rails/scgi_rails-0.4.3.gem
20:22 - http://www.zedshaw.com/downloads/scgi_rails/scgi_rails-0.4.3.gem
        => 'scgi_rails-0.4.3.gem'

Resolving www.zedshaw.com... 67.207.134.146
Connecting to www.zedshaw.com[67.207.134.146]:80... connected.
HTTP request sent, awaiting response... 200 OK
Length: 69,120 [application/octet-stream]

100%
[=====================================================>] 69,120  112.67K/s
20:22:20 (112.59 KB/s) - 'scgi_rails-0.4.3.gem' saved [69,120/69,120]

$ gem install scgi_rails-0.4.3.gem
```

Now, we can change our configuration from `fastcgi.server` to `scgi.server`:

```
modules = ( ..., "mod_scgi", ...)
server.index-files = ("index.html", "index.scgi")
server.error-handler-404 = "/dispatch.scgi"
scgi.server = (
  ".fcgi" => (
    (
      "min-procs" => 1,
      "max-procs" => 5,
      "socket" => "/tmp/rails_scgi.socket",
      "bin-path" => "/www/railsapp/public/dispatch.scgi",
      "docroot" => "/www/railsapp/public"
    )
  )
)
```

With version 1.5.0, spawn-fcgi should also work with SCGI programs, as both interfaces require an application looping forever while listening on a socket.

WordPress

This is a popular blogging software written in PHP. So we can just set it up like most PHP applications. In this example, we will use php-cgi via the FastCGI interface.

To get a FastCGI-compatible PHP, we can either install from source (--with-fastcgi) or let our package manager figure it out. Most distributions will automatically add FastCGI support, if we have the FastCGI packages installed. Gentoo users might want to set the fastcgi use flag. The Windows binaries from http://www.php.net/downloads.php already support FastCGI by default.

Depending on our system, the executable file to use would either be php or php-cgi. The correct executable file should give the following message (here on a windows box):

```
C:\>php-cgi -v
PHP 5.2.6 (cgi-fcgi) (built: May  2 2008 18:02:06)
Copyright (c) 1997-2008 The PHP Group
Zend Engine v2.2.0, Copyright (c) 1998-2008 Zend Technologies
```

The (cgi-fcgi) is the thing to watch out for.

PHP without FastCGI

It is also possible to use PHP without FastCGI support through mod_cgi at a much diminished speed.

Next, we can download WordPress from http://wordpress.org/. The page contains links to the tar.gz and zip packages. We can simply unpack it into our WordPress document root (in this example, in /web/wordpress).

Again, as with most web applications that want to dispatch URLs themselves, we set the error-handler-404 to the provided dispatcher, in this case, /index.php. Also we want to make sure that WordPress' own 404 template gets rewritten to /index.php file in order to make permalinks work. Here is the code:

```
server.modules = ( ..., "mod_rewrite", ... "mod_fastcgi", ...)

$HTTP["host"] == "wordpress.ourdomain.com" {
```

```
server.document-root = "/web/wordpress/"
server.index-files = ("index.html", "index.php")
server.error-handler-404 = "/index.php"
url.rewrite = ("/themes/.*/404.php(\??.*)" => "/index.php$1")
fastcgi.server = (
  ".php" => (
    (
    "min-procs" => 1,
    "max-procs" => 5, # for tuning, see chapter 8.
    "socket" => "/tmp/php-fcgi.socket",
    # alternatively use the spawn-php.sh script that comes
    # with Lighttpd in the doc/ directory.
    "bin-path" => "/usr/bin/php-cgi",
    "docroot" => "/web/wordpress"
    )
  )
)
}
```

Apart from that, we also definitively want to restrict access to the `wp-admin` subdirectory. For this, we can use `mod_access` (refer to Chapter 7) and limit access to valid users:

```
# still within
$HTTP["host"] == "wordpress.ourdomain.com" {
  auth.backend = "htdigest"
  auth.backend.htdigest.userfile = "/etc/lighttpd/wordpress.admin"
  auth.require = (
    "/wp-admin" => (
      "method" => "digest",
      "realm" => "WordPress",
      "require" => "valid-user"
    )
  )
}
```

Refer to Chapter 7 to know how to create `/etc/lighttpd/wordpress.admin` and `/etc/lighttpd/htdigest.userfile`. Now, we can go on to configure our new WordPress blog to our heart's content and start blogging—about how happy are we with our Lighttpd!

phpMyAdmin

As promised in Chapter 7, we will now install phpMyAdmin to work with our Lighttpd. We assume that MySQL is already installed (if not, refer to Chapter 3 for details on installation; also, for PHP setup, see the previous section on Wordpress). Apart from that, phpMyAdmin benefits from two optional PHP extensions.

Extension Name	Description	Usage in phpMyAdmin
GD2	Binds the GD2 graphics library to PHP	Showing inline JPEGs
Mcrypt	Cryptographic library, very advisable	Fast cookie hashing

With that out of the way, let's get phpMyAdmin up and running. If our system has a package manager, we may look if it has a phpMyAdmin package. Otherwise, `http://www.phpmyadmin.net/home_page/downloads.php` has the goods.

We get to choose between English and an International language, and between a stable version and beta version in multiple compressed formats. As far as I can tell, the beta is stable enough. But for this example, we will stick with the stable version, which at the time of this writing is **2.11.9**. After downloading, we can simply unpack the archive into the directory where we want to use phpMyAdmin. For our example, we will use `/web/phpmyadmin`. We should make sure that our PHP processes have read access to the directory, especially if we have a separate **chroot** environment for PHP. For this example, we'll assume the Lighttpd user will be used for PHP as well.

```
mkdir -p /web/phpmyadmin
unzip -d /web/phpmyadmin phpMyAdmin-2.11.9-all-languages.zip
chown -R lighttpd:lighttpd /web/phpmyadmin
```

Next, we need to setup phpMyAdmin. There are two way of doing this. The first way is to create a configuration file in the phpMyAdmin folder. The second way is using a PHP script to create said configuration file. For the latter, skip this section and browse to the setup page at `http://phpmyadmin.ourdomain.com/scripts/setup.php` (change ourdomain.com to your host address) right after configuring your Lighttpd to serve phpMyAdmin.

Myth: phpMyAdmin is a security hole

Using phpMyAdmin will not open our server to anyone, because someone using phpMyAdmin to administrate a database will still need the correct user name and password for the database login and will have restricted access to the database user's rights.

Otherwise, copy the `config.sample.inc.php` to `config.inc.php`, and edit to match our needs. For example, suppose we want to administrate a database on localhost (for example, we might want to have a database table for `mod_mysql_vhost`), we change the `config.inc.php` to:

```php
<?php
$cfg['blowfish_secret'] = '1b63f8c02e5a9827';
// This should be a secret 16-digit hexadecimal number. Should it get
// known, our phpMyAdmin becomes vulnerable to session stealing.
$i=0;
$i++;
// The phpMyAdmin developers suggest using a running variable. This
// way, we cannot make typos causing configuration item mixups.
$cfg['Servers'][$i]['auth_type'] = 'cookie';
$cfg['Servers'][$i]['host'] = 'localhost';
$cfg['Servers'][$i]['connect_type'] = 'tcp';
$cfg['Servers'][$i]['compress'] = false;
// add further code here.
?>
```

This restricts phpMyAdmin to the database server localhost. We can also add a MySQL user and password with the following addition (assuming we use the `root` user with a password of `secret`, change accordingly):

```php
$cfg['Servers'][$i]['user'] = 'root';
$cfg['Servers'][$i]['password'] = 'secret';
```

Note that this implies that anyone having access to the phpMyAdmin will have full access to the database! So to keep this secure, we should add HTTP authentication and serve it only with SSL (given we may want to use it from outside our local network). Now it is time to edit our Lighttpd's configuration. Assuming that we have PHP with FastCGI support (see above), the following will suffice:

```
# mod_auth needed only if MySQL logins are preset
server.modules = ( ..., "mod_access", "mod_auth", "mod_fastcgi", ...)

$HTTP["host"] == "phpmyadmin.ourdomain.com" {
  # uncomment the following if we have finished configuring
    # phpMyAdmin for sensible security:
  # url.access-deny = ("/scripts/setup.php", ".inc.php")
  server.document-root = "/web/phpmyadmin/"
  server.index-files = ("index.html", "index.php")
  fastcgi.server = (
    ".php" => (
      (
```

```
            "min-procs" => 1,
            "max-procs" => 5,
            "socket" => "/tmp/php_fcgi.socket",
            # alternatively use the spawn-php.sh script that comes
            # with Lighttpd in the doc/ directory.
            "bin-path" => "/usr/bin/php-cgi",
            "docroot" => "/web/phpmyadmin"
          )
        )
      )
    # if we need additional security because we have given a MySQL
    # login in our config.inc.php or plan to do so, we should add
    # this:
    $SERVER["socket"] == ":80" {
      # serve only via SSL
      url.redirect = ("(.*)" =>
        "https://phpmyadmin.ourdomain.com/$1")
    }
    auth.backend = "htdigest" # see chapter 7 for creating htdigests.
    auth.backend.htdigest.userfile = "/etc/lighttpd/phpmyadmin.users"
    auth.require = (
      "" => (
        "method" => "digest",
        "realm" => "phpMyAdmin",
        "require" => "valid-user"
      )
    )
  }
```

Now, unless we have postponed configuring our phpMyAdmin because we want
to use the `scripts/setup.php`, uncomment the line denying access to this script.
In either case, make Lighttpd reload its configuration (either by sending a SIGHUP
using `pkill -1 lighttpd` or restarting it).

If we want to configure by using `setup.php`, we first need to create a `config`
directory below `/web/phpmyadmin` (for example, by issuing the following command
to the console:

```
mkdir /web/phpmyadmin/config
```

Browse to `https://phpmyadmin.ourdomain.com/scripts/setup.php`. The following screen will appear:

Note that if we have failed to create the `config` directory, the following error message will appear:

Can not load or save configuration

⚠ Please create web server writable folder config in phpMyAdmin toplevel directory as described in documentation. Otherwise you will be only able to download or display it.

Otherwise, we can set the settings in this dialog and either download the resulting `config.inc.php` to later put it on our server into the `/web/phpmyadmin` directory by clicking on the `download` link or press the `Save` button to save the configuration into the `config`-directory we just created (this is a security measure, by the way). We can then either copy it into the `/web/phpmyadmin` directory or create a link, so that future reconfigurations can take effect immediately, at the cost of some security:

```
cd /web/phpmyadmin
# either
cp config/config.inc.php .
# or
ln config/config.inc.php config.inc.php
```

Now, we better uncomment the `url.access-deny` directive in our `lighttpd.conf`. This way, our phpMyAdmin configuration remains private (see that **Display** button, that could show our configuration to some script kiddie). Restart our Lighttpd again, and we can congratulate ourselves on this fully functional phpMyAdmin.

MediaWiki

MediaWiki is probably not only one of the most popular wiki software today, but also powers Wikipedia, one of the biggest sites today. MediaWiki, like WordPress is a simple PHP application. Well, maybe not on the inside, but the complexity is nicely hidden away from the web server. By the way, Wikipedia uses Lighttpd to power its upload page.

First, download the MediaWiki distribution from the Wikimedia site at `http://download.wikimedia.org/mediawiki`. The latest version at the time of writing is 1.13.0. As MediaWiki relies on PHP, it will run on almost any system that has a fairly recent PHP installed. Unpack the file to a directory, which we will use as the document-root. For our example, it will be `/web/mediawiki`. Make sure this folder is accessible to our PHP process—when in doubt, just run `chown -R lighttpd:lighttpd /web/mediawiki` (or whichever **user:group** combination our PHP process runs with).

For our example, we will assume that our PHP interpreter has FastCGI support; if not, refer to the WordPress section. Now add the following configuration to our `lighttpd.conf`:

```
server.modules = ( ..., "mod_access", "mod_fastcgi", ...)
$HTTP["host"] == "wiki.ourdomain.com" {
  server.document-root = "/web/mediawiki/"
  url.access-deny = ("/config/")
  server.index-files = ("index.html", "index.php")
  server.error-handler-404 = "/index.php"
  fastcgi.server = (
    ".php" => (
      (
      "min-procs" => 1,
      "max-procs" => 5,
      "socket" => "/tmp/php_fcgi.socket",
      # alternatively use the spawn-php.sh script that comes
      # with Lighttpd in the doc/ directory.
      "bin-path" => "/usr/bin/php-cgi",
      "docroot" => "/web/mediawiki"
      )
    )
  )
}
```

Now Lighttpd already serves our Mediawiki. However, we still probably want to configure it. So point your browser to `http://wiki.ourdomain.com/config` to get to the following page:

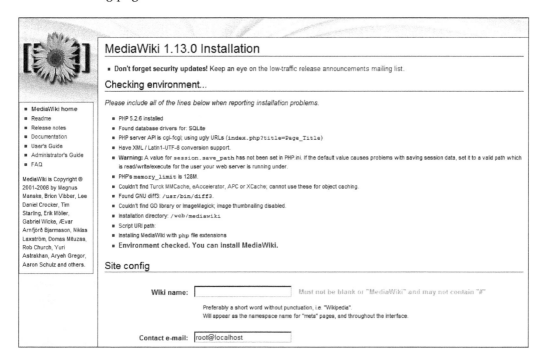

This page shows the MediaWiki environment check and allows us to configure our wiki. Follow the documentation on the site, fill the form, and click the **install MediaWiki** button. Then uncomment the url.access-deny line in our lighttpd.conf to keep the config page private, lest a hacker should reconfigure our wiki.

Depending on the purpose of our wiki, we might add some authentication or other security measures. Refer Chapter 7 for further directions.

Trac

Trac is a wiki and an issue tracker put into a blender and set to 10. Needless to say, it is a great tool for every software project. trac talks FastCGI if we run trac that way. Getting the newest trac version from Subversion seems pretty much a good idea, as the old versions have a lot of dependencies that the trac team removed, but they apparently never got around to releasing a "stable" version since then. The bad news is that we will need a local install of Subversion (look at `http://subversion.tigris.org`). But we can remove it after we have retrieved trac from the repository, or use it integrated with trac.

Setting up trac is a tedious task, even without Lighttpd. So in order to rule out errors we should first set trac up as a standalone server and see if it runs. We can bind it to Lighttpd afterwards.

Authentication with trac

Using trac's authentication is probably a good idea, as it allows us to fine-tune the user permissions. We do not need the `trac-digest.py`, but can use our `htdigest.sh` (refer to Chapter 7 and download the `htdigest.sh` code file from `http://www.packtpub.com/files/code/2103_Code.zip`). Be careful to remember the realm, as we need to give it to `tracd`'s command line. I always use "trac" as realm, to make it easier to remember. However, if we have multiple trac installations, it might be useful to differentiate the realms.

Once we have installed trac, we can set up a project. trac includes a `trac-admin` executable that will allow us to do this in one step with the `initenv` command. For our example, the trac project should reside in `/web/trac/project`.

```
$ trac-admin /web/trac/project initenv
```

Now, we can either run `tracd` as a standalone server and proxy it with Lighttpd or use FastCGI. For the former method, we run `tracd` (let us assume it is on port 8000) as:

```
$ tracd -p 8000 –auth=project,/etc/lighttpd/trac.htdigest,project \
/web/trac/project
```

Optionally we can add a `-s` option so that trac will start with this project directly instead of showing a project list. Now, we can add the following to our `lighttpd.conf`:

```
server.modules = (..., "mod_proxy", ...)
$HTTP["host"] == "trac.ourdomain.com" {
  proxy.server = ("" => ( host => "localhost", port => 8000) )
}
```

Running trac with FastCGI is probably more secure (as we use no network-public port to run the communication between Lighttpd and trac). However, it is a bit more complicated. We create a new file at `/web/trac/trac.fcgi`, which contains the following:

```
#!/usr/bin/python
import os
# either set one project
os.environ['TRAC_ENV'] = "/web/trac/project/"
# or set a parent-dir for multiple projects to get a project list:
#os.environ['TRAC_ENV_PARENT_DIR'] = "/web/trac/"
```

```
# run trac as FastCGI
from trac.web import fcgi_frontend
fcgi_frontend.run()
```

This `trac.fcgi` makes a FastCGI enabled trac out of our normal self-served trac. Now we can summon our FastCGI trac using a modified version of our `lighttpd.conf` snippet used to run MediaWiki:

```
server.modules = ( ..., "mod_access", "mod_fastcgi", ...)

$HTTP["host"] == "trac.ourdomain.com" {
  server.document-root = "/web/trac/project"
  # for multiple projects use "/web/trac" instead.

  url.access-deny = (".ini")
  # disallow access to ini files to keep our configuration private

  server.index-files = ("index.html", "trac.fcgi")
  server.error-handler-404 = "/web/trac/trac.fcgi"
  # track back to the main page if a page is not found

  fastcgi.server = (
    ".fcgi" => (
      (
      "min-procs" => 1, # configure to suit our needs
      "max-procs" => 5,
      "socket" => "/tmp/trac_fcgi.socket",
      # alternatively use the spawn-php.sh script that comes
      # with Lighttpd in the doc/ directory.
      "bin-path" => "/web/trac/trac.fcgi",
      "docroot" => "/web/trac/project"
      )
    )
  )
  # Note that we have a choice between authenticating users by trac
  # or from within Lighttpd. If we choose the latter, see Chapter 7.
}
```

Now, restart Lighttpd and we are right on trac! Sorry, couldn't resist myself ☺. We will see something like this:

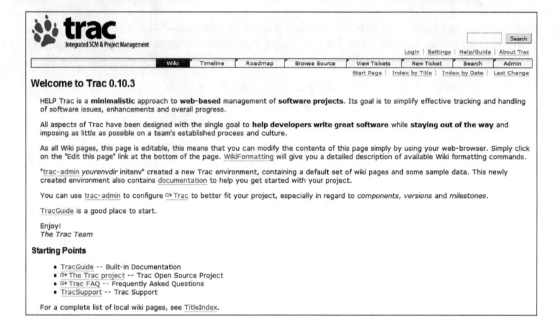

Note that for further trac configuration, edit the per-project configuration in `/web/trac/project/conf/trac.ini` or the global `/usr/share/trac/conf/trac.ini file`. See the trac documentation at `http://trac.edgewall.org/wiki/TracGuide` to check which entries do what.

AWStats

As promised in Chapter 7, here are the steps to get AWStats up and running with our Lighttpd. AWStats requires Perl and a few free kilobytes on our server. As the CGI interface is used only to update the statistics, which should not be done very often (actually once per hour or even per day is usually sufficient), serving AWStats via `mod_cgi` should give us enough performance. However, if we want to use FastCGI (which would remove the setup time for the Perl interpreter sitting in RAM), Chapter 10 has a description on how to port Perl `CGI` to `CGI::FastCGI`.

Now, we can configure AWStats by copying the `awstats.model.conf` to `awstats.ourdomain.conf`. Search the following configuration options and change them to match our Lighttpd configuration (long option names have been split into multiple lines for the sake of brevity, while in the `awstats.ourdomain.conf`, they appear on a single line):

Option name	Description	Value to set (example)
LogFile	This is where the log file should be, depending on our system.	/var/log/lighttpd/access.log C:\Programme\lighttpd\access.log
SiteDomain	The domain for the main site of which log files should be parsed.	www.ourdomain.com
HostAliases	Other names for our domain.	"localhost 127.0.0.1 REGEX[ourdomain\.com$]"
AllowTo UpdateStats FromBrowser	This is one of the long options. If set to 1, it enables the "update" button on the AWStats page.	1
CreateDirData IfNotExists	(Optional) create DirData directory to quell errors if it does not exist.	1

So, for example, we could search for a line with:

```
AllowToUpdateStatsFromBrowser=0
```

and change it to:

```
AllowToUpdateStatsFromBrowser=1
```

This is the minimum change required to make AWStats run on our domain. If we omit the `CreateDirDataIfNotExists` directive, we should create a `DirData` directory below our `/web/awstats` directory (assuming our AWStats is installed at `/web/awstats`):

```
$ mkdir /web/awstats/DirData
```

Finally, we will tell Lighttpd to serve AWStats at `http://awstats.ourdomain.com` with the following configuration:

```
server.modules = ("mod_access", "mod_auth", ... , "mod_cgi", ...)
$HTTP["host"] == "awstats.ourdomain.com" {
  server.document-root = "/web/awstats/wwwroot/"

  # use the perl script if no generated files are there.
  server.error-handler-404 =
    "/web/awstats/wwwroot/cgi-bin/awstats.pl?config=ourdomain"

  url.access-deny = (".pm", ".conf", ".txt")
  # deny web access to modules, config and history files

  cgi.assign = (
    ".pl" => "/usr/bin/perl" # change to wherever your perl is
  )

  # also as the awstats.pl may take some time and other server
  # resources, we want to restrict it to authenticated users
```

```
    auth.backend = "htdigest" # see chapter 7 for creating htdigests.
    auth.backend.htdigest.userfile = "/etc/lighttpd/awstats.users"
    auth.require = (
      "" => (
        "method" => "digest",
        "realm" => "AWStats",
        "require" => "valid-user"
      )
    )
  }
```

Restart Lighttpd (or make it reload the configuration) for the changes to take effect. Browse to http://awstats.ourdomain.com to run AWStats. Note that the canonical URL for running the Perl script is http://awstats.ourdomain.com/cgi-bin/ awstats.pl?config=ourdomain. Click on the **Update** button and rejoice.

AjaxTerm

Setting up AjaxTerm (at the time of this writing, the page was unavailable, but I have version 0.9 lying around) is as simple as this:

```
$ tar xzf AjaxTerm-0.9.tar.gz
$ cd AjaxTerm-0.9
$ configure && make install
Configuring prefix= /usr/local   port= 8022
install -d "/usr/local/bin"
install -d "/usr/local/share/ajaxterm"
install ajaxterm.bin "/usr/local/bin/ajaxterm"
install ajaxterm.initd "/etc/init.d/ajaxterm"
install -m 644 ajaxterm.css ajaxterm.html ajaxterm.js qweb.py sarissa.js
sarissa_dhtml.js "/usr/local/share/ajaxterm"
install -m 755 ajaxterm.py "/usr/local/share/ajaxterm"
gzip --best -c ajaxterm.1 > ajaxterm.1.gz
install -d "/usr/local/share/man/man1"
install ajaxterm.1.gz "/usr/local/share/man/man1"
```

We can now start AjaxTerm as a daemon with the following command line:

```
$ /etc/init.d/ajaxterm start
```

Now, we can browse to http://ourdomain.com:8022/ to see if AjaxTerm is running.

Security Risk

Do not enter any sensitive information here though, as what we send and receive is unencrypted as of now.

AjaxTerm includes its own HTTP server, so we can just proxy it using `mod_proxy`. We also absolutely want to route access to it through SSL, which can be done by the following simple configuration (refer to Chapter 6):

```
server.modules = (..., "mod_redirect", "mod_proxy", ...)
$HTTP["host"] == "ajaxterm.ourdomain.com" {
  $SERVER["socket"] == ":80" {
    url.redirect = ("(.*)" =>
      "https://ajaxterm.ourdomain.com$1")
  }
  proxy.server = ("" => (
    ( "host" => "localhost", "port" => 8022)
  ) )
}
```

We might also want to block access to port 8022 from outside through the use of a firewall, just to be sure. For a thorough rundown of Lighttpd SSL setup, refer Chapter 6.

Otherwise, AjaxTerm is a resource-intensive application. So it deserves to be protected. Otherwise, an attacker could mount a denial-of-service attack by launching a lot of AjaxTerm sessions in parallel.

The most effective solution against this type of attack is restricting it to authenticated users. This can be done with the following code:

```
# from within
$HTTP["host"] == "ajaxterm.ourdomain.com" {
  auth.backend = "htdigest" # see chapter 7 for creating htdigests.
  auth.backend.htdigest.userfile = "/etc/lighttpd/ajaxterm.users"
  auth.require = (
    "" => (
      "method" => "digest",
      "realm" => "AjaxTerm",
      "require" => "valid-user"
    )
  )
  # also as AjaxTerm will make a lot of request, turn the keepalive
  # knob to eleven:
  server.max-keep-alive-requests = 128
  server.max-keep-alive-idle = 10
}
```

We can also use the traffic-shaping abilities of our Lighttpd to limit the possible damage (refer to Chapter 7):

```
# from within
$HTTP["host"] == "ajaxterm.ourdomain.com" {
  # reduce max-write-idle to quit sessions earlier. Note: This may
  # introduce a problem with REALLY slow connections. If we get
  # dropped connections, tune this value up in increments of 10
  # until there are no more errors.
  server.max-write-idle = 60
  # reduce the maximum number of connections so a denial-of-service
  # attack can not bring down the system.
  server.max-connections = 64
}
```

Otherwise, as of version 1.5.0, we would be tempted to use `mod_evasive`. As long as all clients obey the HTTP spec, which limits a client to two parallel connections, this is fine. However, there are some plugins for all popular browsers available which lift this barrier. If we are fine with stopping those people from accessing our AjaxTerm, we can add the following configuration:

```
# add mod_evasive to server.modules
server.modules = (..., "mod_evasive", ...)
# limit to two parallel connections, within
  $HTTP["host"] == "ajaxterm.ourdomain.com" {
  evasive.max-conns-per-ip = 2
}
```

Restart Lighttpd and browse to `ajaxterm.ourdomain.com` to see the following:

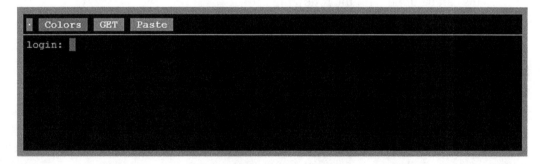

Note that we might use GET after we have entered the login for more speed but less security. As we are running through SSL, this should not be high on our list of concerns anyway.

By the way, someone might be tempted to hack the WSGI-FastCGI bridge from Allan Saddi (you can get it at http://svn.saddi.com/py-lib/trunk/fcgi.py). But using `mod_proxy` is clearly easier, as we do not need to dig into the python code.

Summary

Most web applications and frameworks run with Lighttpd easily by using the FastCGI module. Some rewrite rules, and the right 404 handler will work wonders to keep a nice URL scheme.

Applications that contain their own web servers (such as trac or AjaxTerm) can be handled with `mod_proxy`, perhaps adding SSL and authentication in the process. In this case, we probably want to block direct access to the web application from outside by using a firewall.

Note that there is still a `mod_cgi` to talk to those legacy applications that will not talk FastCGI or SCGI, as well as `mod_ssi` if we have some server-side includes we want to move over from Apache. With version 1.5.0, this will be supplanted by `mod_fastcgi`, which in this version will automatically restart terminated CGI scripts.

12
Using Lua with Lighttpd

Now that we know how to attach most frameworks and applications to Lighttpd, it is time to have a look at a tiny, yet powerful scripting language, which can be used with FastCGI or directly integrated into Lighttpd.

Lua is one of the smallest scripting languages today (the whole distribution still fits on a floppy disk easily), and prides itself on being a meta-paradigm-language.

As of Lighttpd 1.3, a module for cache control added Lua as a programming language. This module was `mod_cml` (**Cache Meta Language**), and its purpose was restricted to control cache operation.

Since Lighttpd 1.4.7, this module has been superseded by `mod_magnet`, which allows Lua to manipulate the request and the reply with no startup cost. Instead it ties up the whole Lighttpd process while the script runs. Alternatively, there is a Lua/FastCGI application, by the author of Lighttpd, which reduces performance only a little, but runs outside the Lighttpd process.

If we have compiled our Lighttpd without Lua, we may now go back to Chapter 1 and add it, or just download the Lua interpreter from `http://www.lua.org` and play around a little bit. The Lua manual can be read online at `http://www.lua.org/manual/5.1`.

Lua: A small Primer

 This section is for coders who want to learn Lua.

Lua is a small, fast, embeddable scripting language. It caters to no particular paradigm, but has simple mechanisms that allow easy implementation of all paradigms. Closures and functions as first-class types serve the functional style, while tables, Lua's swiss-army-knife of data structures, can double up as classes or objects. Co-routines allow turning the program flow inside-out, and an incremental garbage collector keeps the memory requirements low for us. Without further ado, everybody's favorite first program in Lua is:

```
print("Hello, World")
```

This is as unsurprising as most of the languages. Lua has only a few types:

Type	Examples	Description
nil	nil	This is a dummy for anything undefined.
boolean	true, false	Your basic standard boolean values.
number	0, 1, -42, 3.14159	Any number double precision floating point can do.
string	"", 'Hi there', [[\0 multi-line strings]]	Strings can contain escape sequences as in C, but need not be zero-terminated.
function	**function** idle() **end**	Functions are a regular type in Lua. This means we can work with functions as values.
table	{}, {1,2,3},{a="b"}	Tables are the swiss-army-knife collection type of Lua. They work as arrays *and* associative arrays.

In Lua, **all** numbers are stored as double precision floating points. We also have some operators:

Sign(s)	Example	Description
=	a = 1	= does assignment as usual.
== ~= < > <= =>	a == b, x ~= nil, x < y, y > x, a <= b, g => h	~= tests for inequality. All the other relational operators work as usual.
+ - * /	1 + 2 * 3 – 4 / 5	The basic arithmetic operators work as advertised.
^ %	2 ^ 8, x % 7	x^y means x^y (or verbal x to the power of y). x%y is x modulo y (the remainder of a division of x by y).
and or not	a **or** "", x() **and** y	Standard boolean operators. and/or are short-changing: a or b() will not evaluate b() if a is true.
..	"Hello, " .. world	".." concatenates strings (and numbers)
#	#"Hi", #{...}	The length operator. Works on strings and tables (for the latter only based on counting indices).

Operator precedence is borrowed from C (and will usually work as expected). All operators other than % and .. are left-associative.

We can define functions with the `function` keyword. We can `return` multiple values from a function:

```
function x(y) -- This is a comment
  local a = y * y
  return y + 1, a - 1 -- ";" at the end of a statement is optional
end -- [[ This is a multiline comment
          we can use our function as a, b = x(0) ]]
```

The `local` keyword makes a variable scope, local. It is only reachable within the defining block, function, `if`-clause, or loop. Note that we can also define a scope with:

```
do -- [[here is the scope]] end
```

Lua started out as a data description language, but evolved the usual structures to control the program flow:

```
if condition() then block() end

if condition() then block() else block2() end

for i = 1, 3 do block(i) end -- block(1); block(2); block(3)

for i = 1, 5, 2 do block(i) end -- block(1); block(3); block(5)

for key, value in pairs({a="b", b="c"}) do
  io.write(k.."="..v..",") -- pairs is an iterator function.
end -- writes: "a=b,b=c" to standard output

i = 0
while i < 5 do i = i + 1 end -- increment i until 5

repeat i = i + 1 until i > 10 -- and on until 10

while (true) break end -- cheating ourselves out of the infinite loop
```

Most of the power of Lua comes from tables, and this is reflected in the language's design. Tables have their own access operators and their own constructor syntax:

```
a = {} -- creates an empty table

b = {1, "a", function() return 1 end} -- a table used as array
-- as we can see, it can hold objects of any type

c = {a=1, b=2, ["c"]=4, [5]=6} -- both syntaxes for keyed tables

d = {{a=1}, {a=2}, i=function(...) end} -- tables can be nested

e = d[1] -- e == {a=1}; -- Lua counts from one instead of zero!!!

f = d["a"] -- f == nil, note this is also equivalent to f = d.a
-- this also explains while nil can not be a key for a keyed table
```

Lua uses this powerful data structure in many places. Even the global scope is a table, and can be accessed in the runtime as _G, which allows a powerful kind of reflection. As we can see with the fourth example, tables alone are enough to create a kind of object-orientation—a keyed table can encapsulate data and functions. Lua emphasizes this idea by throwing in a bit of syntactic sugar, the implicit self by colon. It has two uses:

```
function mytable:myfunction(a) return self.x + a end
-- function mytable.myfunction(self, a)...
mytable:myfunction(42) -- == mytable.myfunction(mytable, 42)
```

This shorthand for the implicit self makes it easy to distinguish functions that need the self and those that do not. This is the same distinction as that between class and instance methods. But the goodness does not end here: To make tables even more powerful, Lua adds a mechanism called **metatables** that can define the functionality for another table.

Metatable manipulation is done by calling the standard library functions getmetatable and setmetatable:

```
mytable, mymeta = {}, {} -- multi-assignment works, too.
setmetatable(mytable, mymeta)
globmeta = getmetatable(_G) -- yes, we can even mess with _G.
```

Metatables can define a number of functions that are used by the operators:

Description	Meta-Function	How to exercise
Metafunctions for string, table, and function behavior	__len(self)	#self
	__concat(self, x)	self .. x
	__index(self, key)	self[key]
	__setindex(self, key, value)	self[key] = value
	__call(self, ...)	self(...)
Arithmetic functions	__add(self, x)	self + x
	__sub(self, x)	self – x
	__mul(self, x)	self * x
	__div(self, x)	self / x
	__mod(self, x)	self % x
	__pow(self, x)	self ^ x
	__unm(self)	- self
Comparisions (also used for the opposite operator)	__eq(self, x)	self == x (vs. self ~= x)
	__lt(self, x)	self < x (vs. self >= x)
	__le(self, x)	self <= x (vs. self > x)

Metatable.__index can be a table

If the __index entry in the metatable is a table instead of
a function, its entries will mask the table entries of the original table.
For example, given a table t and meta = getmetatable(t) and
meta.__index = {a=1}, then t.a == 1, no matter whether t has
an entry at a or not.

As Lua uses tables for almost everything, and even the metatable of _G, the global
environment can be set. This allows for very flexible redefinition of runtime
behavior. However, for Web programming, some simple functions and tables
holding data usually do this job.

Iterators are another useful feature of Lua. In an above example, we have used
a "for loop" using the built-in ipairs iterator. As the iterator protocol of Lua is
documented, we can write our own iterators. For example, we could replace a
counting "for" loop with the following:

```
function range(f, t)
  return function(_, x) return x<t and x+1 or nil end, nil, f-1
end -- use with: for i in range(1, 10) do ... end
```

Note that our function returns three values: The next() function (which is called
on each iteration), an environment (usually a table, here unused and thus nil,
given as first parameter to our next() function), and the initial variant (the second
parameter). We can also see a common Lua idiom: Using "_" to signify
unused variables.

What Web applications usually need is a way to handle strings. Lua comes only with
a small standard library that does not include Perl Compatible Regular Expressions.
Instead it has its own small regular expression engine with less functionality, more
speed, and a few odd things to note. First, Lua patterns do not use backslashes for
character classes and quoting. Instead the percent sign % is used.

Lua patterns do not allow nested groupings or groupings within multipliers. No
backtracking constructs are included. The usual (refer to Chapter 3) "[...]", "[^...]",
"^", "$", ".", "*", "+" and "?" work, along with "-", which works as the equivalent to
the non-greedy "*?" in PCRE. There is no direct equivalent to the non-greedy "+?". So
in the rare cases where we need it, we may just say "aa-" instead of the "a+?" that we
would use with PCRE.

The following character classes are defined:

%w = [0-9A-Za-z]		%c = [\0-\31]	%p (punctuation)
%x = [0-9A-Fa-f]	%a = [A-Za-z]	%z = [\0]	%s = [\9-\13]
%d = [0-9]	%u = [A-Z] %l = [a-z]	%n = [n] for all n in [^acdluswxz] (quoting)	

For %p, the matched punctuation characters are:
! " § $ % & ' ( ) * + , - . / : ; < = > ? @ [\ ] ^ _ ` { | } ~

Note that for every %e character class there is a %E, which matches the character class and is the opposite.

To match against a string literally using match, we first need to quote it against interpretation by Lua's regex engine. We can do this with the following function:

```
function requote(p)
    return (p or ""):gsub("([%^%$%(%)%%.%[%]%*%+%-%?])", "%%1")
end
```

Here we see a usage of Lua regular expressions: The gsub method replaces all occurrences of a pattern with a replacement string, table, or function (which receives all matched groups as parameters and needs to return a single string replacement). We also see that every string has the string table as index in its metatable, so that mystring:gsub(...) is equivalent to string.gsub(mystring, ...).

Apart from that, Lua has the following string functions:

Name	Example	Description
byte	("ab"):byte(1, 2) == 97, 98	Get the byte values of a string (or part of)
char	string.char(97, 98) == "ab"	Recreate the string by giving the byte values
dump	loadstring(string.dump(f)) == f	Dump a free function (without bound external variables) to a lua-bytecode-string
format	("[%s]"):format("X") == "[X]"	Our usual string formatting function
len	s:len() == #s -- for all s	Get the length of a string
lower	lower("A") == "a"	Change a string to all-uppercase or all-lowercase, respectively
upper	upper("a") == "A"	
rep	("*"):rep(3) == "***"	Repeat a string n times
sub	("Hello"):sub(0, 4) == "Hell"	Take a substring (second argument is optional)
reverse	("dooG"):reverse() == "Good"	Reverse a string

These 14 functions are enough for advanced text processing. And if they are not enough, we can get access to more functions by using modules, written either in Lua or C/C++.

The module system of Lua has undergone some changes in the last versions. Earlier, Lua versions just had a "loadfile" built-in function. Now if we want to load a module, we can do so with `require("mymodule")`. Lua will then search the two tables of paths for Lua (`package.path`) and C modules (`package.cpath`), and load the first available. It also keeps track of the already loaded modules, so we may need `require()` twice without any problem. We can also create our own modules in Lua. The module-function will reserve a fresh namespace for us:

```
module("mymodule")
```

We can also add an arbitrary number of functions to be applied over our newly-created module namespace. For example, the `package.seeall` function will set the metatable of our namespace to a table such as { __index = _G }. Just use it with:

```
module("mymodule", package.seeall)
```

Useful Lua Libraries

`require()` allows us to add functionality by loading C libraries at runtime (given that we have compiled with dynamic linking, refer to Chapter 1). We can already do some stuff with the standard distribution, but there is no support for advanced file system operation, databases, imaging, network programming, and so on. The following libraries should fill the biggest gaps:

- **LuaFileSystem** (`http://keplerproject.org/luafilesystem`): This library is of interest if we want to manage files from within Lua. It contains functions to iterate through directories, work with symbolic links, and file locking.

- **LuaSQL** (`http://keplerproject.org/luasql`): This connects to and works with a number of SQL databases, including Oracle, MySQL, SQLite and PostgreSQL.

- **MD5** (`http://www.keplerproject.org/md5/`): This is another useful library from project Kepler, adding an often-used hash function to our repertoire.

- **LuaSocket** (`http://www.tecgraf.puc-rio.br/~diego/professional/luasocket`): This gives Lua networking capabilities and includes implementations of HTTP/FTP/SMTP clients and some other helper classes to work with MIME messages, URLs, and so on, on top of a low-level TCP/IP and UDP core.

- **Lua-GD** (`http://lua-gd.luaforge.net`): This is a binding to the popular GD graphics library. We may use it to generate graphics dynamically.

Apart from those, the Lua-users wiki (`http://lua-users.org/wiki`) has a lot of sample code and extensions. There is also LuaForge (`http://luaforge.net`), a Lua project site.

Lua/FastCGI

The Lua/FastCGI interface comes as a single C file. It simply embeds the Lua interpreter, binding it to the FastCGI interface, adding a little functionality here and there. The result is that 223 lines of C code create a fully functional FastCGI scripting environment, including a byte code cache, Lighttpd's stat cache and GET and POST processing capabilities.

Installing Lua/FastCGI

We can get it from `http://jan.kneschke.de/projects/lua`. If we have already installed Lua and FastCGI (refer to Chapter 1, if not); we can compile it using `gcc` with:

```
$ gcc -Wall -O2 -g -o magnet magnet.c -lfcgi -llua -lm -ldl -Wl,-E
```

Why the `-Wl,-E`? The site says nothing about it?

The `-Wl` option gives a list of comma-separated options to the linker. The `-E` linker option can also be written as "–export-dynamic" and tells the linker to export all symbols as dynamic. If we omit this option, our Lua scripts will not be able to find any C function, including all the built-in functions! Also be sure to compile Lua with dynamic linking support, so we can use Lua libraries.

Then we may put the magnet executable in a suitable place. Most Linux distributions will want it in `/usr/local/bin` or `/usr/bin`. If we run Lighttpd in a chroot (refer to Chapter 8), we may start magnet inside or outside the chroot, provided the socket used is reachable from Lighttpd. Note that a big reason given in Chapter 8 for separating Lighttpd from the backend does not usually apply here: Lua/FastCGI is neither big nor complex (however, your applications might be written in it).

To make Lighttpd talk to our Lua/FastCGI applications, we add the following into our `lighttpd.conf` file (or somewhere included from there):

```
server.modules = ( #...
  "mod_fastcgi", # make sure we include mod_fastcgi
  #...
)
server.index-files = ("index.html", "index.lua")
fastcgi.server = (
  ".lua" => (
    ("socket" => "/tmp/lua-fcgi.socket",
     "bin-path" => "/usr/local/bin/magnet",
     "max-procs" => 8 )
  )
)
```

Now we can start with our first Lua website. Put the following into the `index.lua` file, in a directory below the document root (let us say luatest):

```
print([[Status: 200
Content-Type: text/html

<html>
  <head>
    <title>
        Congratulations!
    </title>
  </head>
<body>
  Lua appears to work.
</body></html>]])
```

If we have compiled Lua/FCGI without error and configured Lighttpd correctly, browsing http://localhost/luatest/ should now say: "Lua appears to work."

As we can see, we have complete control over the headers, so we can send different HTTP status codes (for a complete definition of HTTP status codes see Appendix A or `http://www.w3.org/Protocols/rfc2616/rfc2616-sec10.html`), which can be quite interesting depending on our application. For example, sending a status of '204 No Content' if a dynamic site is unchanged will make the browser stay at the same page after a POST request. Also, we can set the Content-Length, which we either know before or collect by intercepting the print function:

```
header = {["Content-Type"]="text/html"}
content = {}
size = 0
_print = print
function print(...)
  for _, v in pairs({...}) do
    local tmp = tostring(v)
    size = size + #tmp
    table.insert(content, tmp)
  end
end
function out()
  header["Content-Length"] = size + #content -- for newlines
  for k, v in pairs(header) do _print(k .. ": " .. v) end
  print("\n")
  for _, v in ipairs(content) do _print(v) end
end
```

Now calling the print to output content will collect it to be printed out by the out function, which we can call at the end of our script. This code just outlines the basic idea (for example we might want to intercept `io.write`), but can be extended easily.

Manipulating the headers will also allow us to set Cookies, to create a session, for example:

```lua
require("md5") -- from Kepler
require("mime") -- from LuaSocket

local sessionId = os.getenv("HTTP_COOKIE"):match("$id=[^&]*")

if sessionId == nil then
  sessionId = mime.b64(md5.sum(os.getenv("REMOTE_ADDRESS")..
    tostring(math.random())
  header["Set-Cookie"] = "id="..sessionId..";maxAge=3600"
end
```

We can then use this `sessionId` as key for a session table to store per-user data for our Web application.

GET and POST Requests

It is good that now, we can let Lua write our pages, but we could also want to parse the request for user input, so we can react to forms, file uploads, and so on. The easiest form of request is a GET request: after the page URL and a "?" (or similar separator) comes a "&" separated list of uri-encoded key=value pairs, which for FastCGI scripts is usually in the QUERY_STRING environment variable. The following code takes this environment variable and puts the uri-decoded key-values into a table:

```lua
local function uridecode(k)
return (k or ""):gsub("[\r%+]",
{['\r']='\n', ["+"]=" "}):gsub("%%(%x%x)", function(h)
return string.char(tonumber(h,16))
end)
end

get, q = {}, os.getenv("QUERY_STRING") or ""

for k, v in q:gmatch("([^&=]+)=([^&=]*)") do
  get[uridecode(k)] = uridecode(v)
end
```

Let us see what happens here. The `uridecode` function uses two little known features of `string.gsub`. For replacement, it can take a table or even a function that is called for each match with the matched groupings as arguments. The other code just creates a table called `get` and iterates over the matches of the query string with a key=value pattern, calling `uridecode` to sanitize the keys and values before putting them in the table.

Reading POST requests is a wee tiny bit more complicated, as the request content is read from the standard input. However, we may not read more than the content length, lest our script will block, waiting for more bytes from the client, which of course never arrive.

The easiest (and most carefree) way to read a "normal" form POST (using the `uridecode` function discussed earlier) is as follows:

```
post, q = {}, io.read(os.getenv("CONTENT_LENGTH") or 0)
for k, v in q:gmatch("([^&=]+)=([^&=]*)") do
  post[uridecode(k)] = uridecode(v)
end
```

If we got a terabyte-sized POST request, this would actually try and read it into the memory, bringing down the Lua/FastCGI, and maybe even freeze the whole system.

A more careful algorithm tries to read only as much bytes of the request as needed and will write the data out into temporary files if there is more data than we want to have in memory. Remember iterators? They come in handy, here:

```
function iterpost()
  return function(e, _)
    readUntilMatches(e, kv) -- key-value-separator
    key = e.buf:match(e.b .. "(.-)" .. kv)
    if key == nil then return nil end
    e.buf = e.buf:match(kv .. "(.*)")

    readUntilMatches(e, e.b) -- boundary
    value = e.buf:match("(.-)" .. e.b)
    e.buf = e.buf:sub(#value)

    return uridecode(key:match('name="(.-)"')), uridecode(value)
  end,
    { -- the initial environment e for the above function
        bytes=tonumber(os.getenv("CONTENT_LENGTH") or 0),
        b="\n" .. requote((os.getenv("CONTENT_TYPE")
        or ""):match("boundary=(%S*)")), kv="\r?\n\r?\n", buf=""
    }
end
```

Now this is some dense code (even with the empty lines sprinkled here and there), but it just basically reads blocks of data until it matches the next key, then further until it matches the next value, and so on. We use the `requote` and the `uridecode` functions we have defined earlier. The `readUntilMatches` function is trivially defined as follows:

```
function readUntilMatches(e, b)
    while e.bytes > 0 and not e.buf:match(b) do
        bytes = math.min(e.bytes, 8192)
        -- using buffersize of 8192 bytes
        e.buf = e.buf .. io.read(bytes)
        e.bytes = e.bytes - bytes
    end
end
```

> This solution still takes everything into memory, even if only in steps. However, it is possible (if not simple) to add code that puts values that are bigger than our chunk size of 8192 directly into temp files. This code was omitted for brevity, but is part of a `cgi` module you can download the `cgi.lua` file from `http://www.packtpub.com/files/code/2103_Code.zip`.

Looking at the Cache

Lua/FastCGI keeps a bytecode cache within Lua, so we can access the internals. The cache is simply a table with script names as keys and more tables as values, each of which has the following entries:

Entry	Example	Description
mtime	1196199674	When the entry was cached in Lua's `os.time()` format
hits	27	The number of hits since this entry was cached
script	function (0xf85a71b)	The compiled and cached bytecode as a Lua function

Note that these are plain Lua tables, and they are not even write-protected. This means we can force a reload of the script `myscript` with the following command:

```
magnet.cache["myscript"] = { mtime=os.time(), hits=1,
    script=loadfile("myscript.lua") } -- or loadstring or function
```

Also reading the table gives us a good idea about pages, which have been requested most often and they may be good targets for optimization (refer to Chapter 9).

We have now everything we need to create Web applications with Lua/FastCGI. On to `mod_magnet`!

Running mod_magnet

Having Lua embedded in the server means there is no redirection, no interprocess communication, and nothing to keep us from killing our Lighttpd if our code hangs. For this section, we should have installed mod_magnet in Chapter 1 (if not, go back there and reinstall). Now add the following to the configuration:

```
server.modules = ( #...
  "mod_magnet", #...
)
# either of the following two:
magnet.attract-raw-url-to = ( "/path/to/my.lua" )
magnet.attract-physical-path-to = ( "/path/to/other.lua" )
```

The first option will invoke the magnet before Lighttpd has even inferred the physical path. We are operating directly on URLs. This is a good option if we want to code complex rewrite logic in Lua. The other option will hand the parsed request to our Lua script, which is fine when we want to manipulate the response.

mod_magnet gives us some hints at the request and environment, and some means to manipulate the request and the response. When our magnet script starts, the following tables are populated:

```
lighty={
  ["RESTART_REQUEST"]=99, -- A constant for returning to Lighttpd
  header={ --[[ The headers go here ]] },
  request={
    ["Accept"]="text/xml,application/xml,application/xhtml+xml," ..
"text/html;q=0.9,text/plain;q=0.8,image/png,*/*;q=0.5",
    ["Accept-Charset"]="ISO-8859-1,utf-8;q=0.7,*;q=0.7",
    ["Accept-Encoding"]="gzip,deflate",
    ["Accept-Language"]="en-us;q=0.8,en-en;q=0.5,en;q=0.3",
    ["Host"]="mydomain.com",
    ["User-Agent"]="Mozilla/5.0 ..."
  },
  env={ --[[ Depends on if we attract raw url or physical path ]] },
  content={ --[[ The content goes here ]] },
  status={ --[[ A table for mod_status/collecting statistics ]] },
  stat=function(filename) ... end
}
```

print(...) will go straight to the Lighttpd error log for us to read.

stat(...) returns a table with the following quite self-describing entries: is_file, is_dir, is_char, is_block, is_socket, is_link, is_fifo, st_mtime, st_ctime, st_atime, st_uid, st_gui, st_size, st_ino, etag, content-type.

Here are the contents of the `lighty.env` table on a normal request with `magnet.attract-raw-url` set:

```
lighty.env = {
  ["uri.path"]="/path/to/file.html"
  ["uri.path-raw"]="/path/to/file.html"
  ["uri.scheme"]="http"
  ["uri.authority"]="mydomain.com"
  ["request.uri"]="/path/to/file.html"
  ["request.orig-uri"]="/path/to/file.html"
}
```

Note that no rewriting took place. If it did, `request.uri` and `request.orig-uri` might differ. If we use `magnet.attract-physical-path`, we get the following additional entries:

```
lighty.env = { ... -- see above
  ["physical.path"]="/var/www/docroot/path/to/file.html"
  ["physical.rel-path"]="/path/to/file.html"
  ["physical.doc-root"]="/var/www/docroot"
}
```

Now what to do with all these tables? The simple thing to do is to set headers and content to be sent out by Lighttpd. So let us try it. We carve out a niche at our server where we want to test mod_magnet by including it into our `lighttpd.conf` file:

```
server.modules = ( #...
  "mod_magnet", #...
  # make sure it is there, for example right after mod_access

  )


$HTTP["host"] == "magnet.ourdomain.com" {
  server.document-root = "/path/to/docroot"
  magnet.attract-physical-path-to = "/path/to/docroot/test.lua"
}
```

Now, we will put the following into our /path/to/docroot/test.lua:

```
lighty.headers = { ["Document-Type"] = "text/html" }
lighty.content = {"<html><head><title>mod_magnet</title></head>",
  "<body>It's alive!</body></html>"}
return 200
```

Now point your browser at http://magnet.ourdomain.com—you should be greeted by **It's alive**. This example shows that we can put as many strings into lighty.content as we want. Lighttpd will send them out one by one. We also can include files. For example, if we had a README file in the document root, we could have it sent as a HTML file with:

```
lighty.headers = { ["Document-Type"] = "text/html" }
local root = lighty.env["physical.doc-root"]
lighty.content = {"<html><head><title>README</title></head><body>",
  "<pre>", {filename=root.."README"}, "</pre></body></html>"}
return 200
```

Yes, that's all. When mod_magnet encounters a table within the lighty.content table, it will look for its filename field and include the named file. Note that in conjunction with luafilesystem, we can use this to collect all files that match some description and let Lighttpd put them together easily. Or we can add a standard header and footer onto all the sites with all the fancy stuff that Lua lets us do.

Another use for mod_magnet is rewriting and redirecting. Although mod_rewrite and mod_redirect do a good job for us, there are things they will not do, like rewriting a URL to the first file found by a search or rewriting based on the time of day or a random number. All these things can be done with mod_magnet and a little Lua code. But first, let us dissect a simple mod_magnet rewrite:

```
lighty.env["request.uri"] = string.gsub(
  lighty.env["request.uri"] or "", "foo", "bar")
return lighty.RESTART_REQUEST
```

This code is changing the request URI and telling Lighttpd to restart the request handling. Now a simple redirect looks like this:

```
lighty.header["Location"] = string.gsub(
  lighty.env["request.uri"] or "", "foo", "bar")
return 302 -- moved temporarily
```

Both snippets work if included with magnet.attract-raw-url-to. Now on to more complex examples:

```
-- redirect to first found
if lighty.stat(lighty.env["uri.path"]) == nil then
  searchPatterns = {"media/?", "other/?", "cache/?"}
  for _, v in ipairs(searchPatterns) do
    local path = string.gsub(v, "%?", lighty.env["uri.path"])
    if lighty.stat(path) ~= nil then
      lighty.request["Location"] = path
      return 302
    end
  end
  return 404
end
```

Included with `magnet.attract-physical-path-to`, it will redirect to the first file found (if the file that was requested was not there in the first place) using the `searchPatterns` or send a `404` file not found response if it finds no files.

Other possible uses include rewriting to a `random` file:

```
-- rewrite based on random number
dir = "/var/www/random/"
files = {"a.png", "x.png", "not.png", "else.png"}
lighty.header["Content-Type"] = "image/png"
lighty.content = {{filename=dir .. files[math.random(#files)]}}
return 200
```

Of course, we will want to change `dir` and `files` to suit our needs. Note that the number we generate here with `math.random` can come from any source, so we may serve files based on the time of day, the contents of the various header fields or any other data we can imagine.

We might want to re-read the directory and the list of files from a file at runtime. As the global environment _G changes only on restart of Lighttpd, we can use it as a cache and use `lighty.stat` to know when to reload (here extending our preceding example):

```
-- caching file contents in _G
source = "/var/www/random/files"
if _G.filecache == nil or
    lighty.stat(source).st_mtime > _G.filecache.time then
  _G.filecache = {time=os.time()}
  for f in io.lines(source) do
    if f ~= nil and f:gsub("%s", "") ~= "" then
      table.insert(_G.filecache, (f or ""):gsub("%s*$", ""))
    end
  end
end
-- now we can use _G.filecache as our "files" list as above.
```

Note that we might want to use a prefix of the name of the running script so as not to overwrite the namespace of other magnet scripts. Also this caching can be used for about everything, from lists of files to html snippets to search paths to rewrite rules, for example, stored as a line containing `pattern => replacement` per rule.

Example: A Shoutbox

In the following example, we will exercise both the Lua Magnet and `mod_magnet` to create a **shoutbox**, a list of messages into which users can enter plain text. Only the ten newest messages are shown.

The basic idea is that reading is done more often than shouting, is probably a fast operation and can be cached, so we will use `mod_magnet` to assemble the shoutbox. Shouting, on the other hand, involves validating a message against Cross-site scripting attacks, writing it to a file, and possibly removing old messages. This will be done using the Lua magnet.

The basic layout will be as follows:

Page name	Description
`/index.lua`	The mod_magnet script to assemble the shoutbox
`/.header.html.inc`	A header to add to the shoutbox
`/.footer.html.inc`	A footer to add to the shoutbox
`/shout.lua`	The Lua magnet script to add a message
`/messages/`	The directory in which to store the messages
`/messages/8783608325`	A sample message named by 999999999 − timestamp

To get a feeling of what we are trying to accomplish, look at the following picture. The complete shoutbox should look like this:

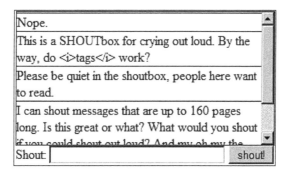

Create the necessary directories and make the messages directory writable to our Lua magnet, so `shout.lua` can write messages. Our example will be located in `/web/shoutbox`, so enter the following commands (assuming a UNIX system):

```
$ mkdir -p /web/shoutbox/messages
$ chown lighttpd:lighttpd /web/shoutbox/messages
```

Starting with a HTML mock-up (which when rendered looks like the preceding picture), we can easily extract `.header.html.inc`:

```
<html>
<head>
<title>Shoutbox</title>
<style type="text/css">
.shoutBox { width:20em; height:10em; overflow:auto;
border:1px solid #777; padding:0px; }
.shoutBox p { display:block; width:100%; border-top:1px solid #700;
margin:1px 0px; }
</style>
</head>
<body>
<div class="shoutBox"><p>
```

Save the file in `/web/shoutbox/.header.html.inc`. The messages are separated by `</p><p>`, which we will later use directly in `index.lua`. Now, we can extract everything below the shouted messages into `.footer.html.inc`:

```
</p></div>
<form name="Shoutbox" action="shout" method="POST">
Shout: <input type="text" name="s" size="32" maxlength="160" />
<input type="submit" value="shout!" />
</form>
</body>
</html>
```

Save this file into `/web/shoutbox/.footer.html.inc`. Between the previous two HTML pieces, the `index.lua` will concatenate the contents of all the files in the `messages` directory, with a separator between each, add the header and footer, and send it out. We use the fact that on all tested systems `lfs.dir()` sorts the filenames in alphabetical order to save on sorting (we could have done it with `table.sort(...)` else). The code is simple enough:

```
-- index.lua: put the shoutbox together.
require("lfs") -- use LuaFileSystem

lighty.headers = { ["Document-Type"] = "text/html" }
lighty.content = {{filename=".header.html.inc"}}

local root = lighty.env["physical.doc-root"]
for name in lfs.dir("messages") do
  if name ~= "." and name ~= ".." then -- add to lighty.content
    table.insert(lighty.content, {filename=root..name})
```

```
      table.insert(lighty.content, "</p><p>" -- our separator
   end
end

table.insert(lighty.content, {filename=".footer.html.inc"}}

return 200
```

Now we just need the messages to appear in the `messages` directory. This will be done by using `shout.lua`. This script has to do the following:

1. Read.

2. Parse the message (in our example, we will just be using HTML-encode < >, &, and ").

3. Write it to a file (we will prepare a code file using a simple formula which will ensure that newer messages come first in alphabetical order).

4. Count the number of files and look whether it is greater than 10.

5. Delete the oldest file (if there are more than 10 entries).

6. Send a redirect to the index page.

Here is the code that performs this task step by step:

```
-- shout.lua: save a message into the messages directory, clean up
-- old messages
require("cgi") -- use the CGI module we created before
require("lfs") -- and the LuaFileSystems module

local numberofmessages = 10
local messagepath = "messages/"
-- 1. read message
local message = cgi.post["s"]
if message ~= nil then
  -- 2. parse message: Encode HTML tags
  message = message:gsub("[<>&\"]",
    {"<"="&lt;", ">"="&gt;", "&"="&amp;", '"'="&quot;"})

  -- 3. write message to file
  local filename = 9999999999 - os.time()
  local messagefile = io.open(messagepath .. filename))
  messagefile:write(message)
  messagefile:close()
end
```

```lua
-- 4. count files
local files = {}
for file in lfs.dir() do
  if file ~= "." and file ~= ".." then
    table.insert(files, file)
  end
end

if #files > numberofmessages then    -- 5. delete last file
  os.remove(messagepath .. files[#files])
end

-- 6. redirect to main page
print([[Status: 302
        Location: /]])
```

The Lua code is in place, so we can edit our Lighttpd configuration to make the magnet attract the main directory to the shoutbox. Rewrite /shout to /shout.lua so the form will have a valid target. Then make shout.lua served by Lua magnet and put the whole thing on its own domain. Here is the code:

```
server.modules = ( "mod_access", "mod_rewrite", "mod_magnet",
  "mod_fastcgi" )

$HTTP["host"] == "shoutbox.ourdomain.com" {
  url.access-deny = ( ".header.html.inc", ".footer.html.inc",
    "/messages/" )
  url.rewrite = ( "^shout$" => "shout.lua" )
  fastcgi.server = (
  ".lua" => (
    ("socket" => "/tmp/lua-fcgi.socket",
     "bin-path" => "/usr/local/bin/magnet",
     "max-procs" => 2 ) # will be enough
    )
  )
  $HTTP["url"] ~= "^/?$" {
    magnet.attract-physical-path = ( "index.lua" )
  }
}
```

Finally, we have the configuration, so we can restart Lighttpd and have fun shouting into the shoutbox. By the way, feel free to use this code on your own site. The shoutbox might be a very simple example, but the underlying method can be extended to create a blog with comments, an AJAX live chat, or things that we can't even yet imagine.

Summary

Lua is a very powerful language and ideally suited for use with Lighttpd. While it will probably not supersede the traditional Web scripting languages (most of which begin with a "P"), its stable implementation, high-speed, and low-memory footprint makes it a great addition to our tool chest.

mod_magnet has the advantage of zero startup cost plus access to Lighttpd's stat cache implementation, at the price of stopping all other server tasks of this process while the scripts run. Therefore, it should be used only for very small tasks (like smart caching, picking a file or slapping a header and footer on a site). Also mod_magnet is probably the best tool out there for coding complex and dynamic rewrites.

For bigger tasks, Lua/FastCGI will have very little startup cost (compared to other Web scripting languages), while still giving us the whole power of Lua in a FastCGI environment. The added socket between Lua and Lighttpd costs little, performance-wise. And the low-memory footprint means that we need little memory per process, so we can ramp up the number of processes to distribute the workload.

With a combination of both these techniques, we can keep our site simple and fast, as showcased in the shoutbox example. However, when mixing Lua magnet and mod_magnet code, we have to be careful about the differences. With mod_magnet, we have the lighty-table and return the status code, while Lua magnet scripts have the magnet-table instead, and have to write the HTTP headers without outside help, but unlike mod_magnet can be persuaded to parse POST-requests.

The dynamic nature of Lua makes it simple to gloss over some small differences, but we are still unable to move code from mod_magnet to the Lua magnet or vice versa. So, we can be thankful about having both in our toolbox.

13
Writing Lighttpd Modules

Lighttpd is built to be small. It also strives to give all the needed functionality for a variety of applications. As different users tend to have different needs, it is only logical that Lighttpd is extensible with modules. To keep this module small, the module interface is quite simple. Modules get the full benefit of the Lighttpd configuration file parser, so they do not need to create their own. This also keeps the configuration syntax for modules consistent.

Modules live directly in the server. They are usually written in C (Lighttpd requires a C binding, which could be done with C++ or other languages, but in practice rarely is), so they are faster than using mod_magnet (which is already pretty fast). The downside is that writing a module is much more tedious and error-prone than writing a Lua script for use with mod_magnet. This brings us to the following rule of thumb:

Do not write a module where a mod_magnet script will do

A mod_magnet script is usually smaller and much easier to write. The higher level of abstraction leaves less chances of making mistakes. C, unlike Lua, leaves the memory handling to the programmer. Also the standard string-handling functions open security holes when used improperly. Even if we are hell-bent on writing a module, it makes sense to write a prototype mod_magnet script first, presuming, of course, that the function is possible to implement in Lua.

Now that it is out of the way, we can start writing modules. First, we will implement the famous "Hello, World" program as a Lighttpd module:

```
#includes "base.h"
#includes "log.h"
#includes "plugin.h"

#ifdef HAVE_CONFIG_H
```

```
#includes "config.h"
#endif

typedef struct { PLUGIN_DATA; /* no config */ } plugin_data;

INIT_FUNC(mod_helloworld_init) {
  plugin_data *p;
  UNUSED(srv);
  p = calloc(1, sizeof(*p));
  log_trace("Hello, World!");
  return p;
}

FREE_FUNC(mod_helloworld_free) {
  plugin_data *p = p_d;
  UNUSED(srv);
  if (p) free(p);
  return HANDLER_GO_ON;
}

int mod_helloworld_plugin_init(plugin *p) {
  p->version = LIGHTTPD_VERSION_ID;
  p->name = buffer_init_string("helloworld");
  p->init = mod_helloworld_init;
  p->cleanup = mod_helloworld_free;
  p->data = NULL;
  return 0;
}
```

This is the absolute minimum for a module, and it does nothing very useful. It only logs "Hello, World" when loaded. However, by compiling, linking, and running mod_helloworld.c from within Lighttpd, we can see if our toolchain works as expected.

We presumably use a POSIX-compliant development system. If not, we may need to make a few changes to the following command lines to make them work.

Before we test our module, let us have a look at the source code. Apart from some boiler plate (the #include) we have a type definition for the plugin data (we just use the predefined PLUGIN_DATA, which just contains an id for our plugin) and three functions.

The `mod_helloworld_plugin_init` function is called directly after loading the module. Then Lighttpd calls the `mod_helloworld_init` function to obtain a `plugin_data`. Note that we need to return something that at least holds a `PLUGIN_DATA` (which is conveniently the first element in our `plugin_data` structure). When Lighttpd finishes, it calls `mod_helloworld_free` to release the memory held by `plugin_data`. Beware that not freeing the `plugin_data` creates a memory hole. The `UNUSED(srv);` line tells the C compiler that it is possible to optimize away the variable (`UNUSED` is a macro defined in `buffer.h`). It is not strictly needed, but a good style to include, and may also reduce warnings on some compilers.

All functions except `mod_helloworld_init` (for obvious reasons) return an integer value, usually the one defined in `settings.h`. We need to be careful with the return values. All functions that are called when Lighttpd gets started may return `HANDLER_ERROR` on failure, which will stop Lighttpd immediately. Other functions are usually called per connection, so they should not return `HANDLER_ERROR` at all. However, if they did, they would be shutting down Lighttpd every time the error condition occurs. If there is an error during processing a connection, the correct action is to set the HTTP status to 500 (internal server error) and return `HANDLER_FINISHED` (unless we want a module for auto-shutdown):

```
con->http_status = 500;
return HANDLER_FINISHED;
```

If we do not want to finish the processing (for example, see the `mod_helloworld_free` function), we can easily return `HANDLER_GO_ON`. Note that if a `mod_*_free` function returned `HANDLER_FINISHED`, it would stop processing the "free" request, opening the dreaded memory hole once again.

To test our module, we compile it first. The easiest way to do that is when we have the `mod_helloworld.c` in the `src` directory of a Lighttpd source distribution. If we do not have one, we can download the package from `http://www.lighttpd.net` and unpack it.

Then from the `src` directory, we can just do the following (lines with `$` are console inputs):

```
$ make mod_helloworld.o
if gcc -DHAVE_CONFIG_H -DLIBRARY_DIR="\"/usr/local/lib\"" -I. -I. -
I..  -D_REENTRANT -D__EXTENSIONS__  -D_FILE_OFFSET_BITS=64 -D_LARGEFILE_
SOURCE -D_LARGE_FILES -pthread -I/usr/include/glib-2.0 -I/usr/lib/glib-
2.0/include  -g -O2 -Wall -W -Wshadow -pedantic -std=gnu99 -MT mod_
helloworld.o -MD -MP -MF ".deps/mod_helloworld.Tpo" -c -o mod_helloworld.
o mod_helloworld.c; \
        then mv -f ".deps/mod_helloworld.Tpo" ".deps/mod_helloworld.Po";
```

```
else rm -f ".deps/mod_helloworld.Tpo"; exit 1; fi
$ gcc -shared -o mod_helloworld.so mod_helloworld.o
ld: warning: creating a DT_TEXTREL in object.
$ # hooray, it compiled
```

Now we can install our module into the installation directory (presuming that we've kept the default module installation directory of /usr/local/lib, change if necessary):

```
$ /usr/bin/install -c mod_helloworld.so /usr/local/lib/mod_helloworld.so
$
```

Now we are ready to include our mod_helloworld into our lighttpd.conf:

```
    server.modules = ("mod_helloworld", ...)
```

When we run our Lighttpd with the lighttpd.conf, we should see the following (change the path to lighttpd.conf if needed):

```
$ /usr/local/sbin/lighttpd -D -f /etc/lighttpd/lighttpd.conf
Hello, World!
```

Note that after the module_init function has finished, all trace output goes to the Lighttpd error.log file.

So far, so good. Now let's get on to something more demanding. For most module implementations we will at least need some configuration. This is easily done by extending the plugin_data type definition and augmenting the mod_init and mod_free functions with the needed memory handling. Apart from that, a few other functions are supplied to deal with configuration handling.

Handling Configuration

Most modules define a plugin_config data type, so they can re-use it from within the plugin_data type. For each selector clause, Lighttpd opens a new configuration context. Therefore, we need an array with one plugin_config for each context. This array will be filled by the mod_*_setdefaults function, and needs to be freed by the mod_*_free function. The usual configuration types are buffer and array, defined in buffer.h and array.h, respectively (we do not need to include them, as they are already included in base.h).

Let us just add some configuration to our example. Here is a selection of possible configuration values:

```
typedef struct {
  unsigned short boolean_value; /* e.g. our.fun=enable */
  unsigned short short_value; /* e.g. our.port=80 */
  unsigned int int_value; /* wherever we may need one */
  buffer *string_value; /* e.g. we.love="Lighttpd" */
  array *array_value; /* e.g. our.array=("a", "b") or ("a"=>"b") */
  /* be sure to include buffer.h and array.h */
} plugin_config;
```

Now we add this `plugin_config` to our `plugin_data` — once directly for the global context and once in an array per context, to allow multiple contexts:

```
typedef struct {
  PLUGIN_DATA;
  plugin_config **config_storage;
  plugin_config conf;
} plugin_data;
```

A context is created by each selector, including `else`-clauses. This is the secret to the power of Lighttpd's configuration system, because it allows us to carve out sections where configuration may differ from the global configuration.

We also need to add a new set of default functions (SETDEFAULTS_FUNC) to get the configuration from the `lighttpd.conf` file into our `plugin_config`. Also, we should be nice to the environment and clean up our configuration in the `mod_*_free` function:

```
FREE_FUNC(mod_helloworld_free) {
  plugin_data *p = p_d;
  UNUSED(srv);
  if (!p) return HANDLER_GO_ON;
  if (p->config_storage) {
    size_t i;
    for (i = 0; i < srv->config_context->used; i++) {
      plugin_config *s = p->config_storage[i];
      if (!s) continue;
      /*  we need to free string/array values with the
        respective function */
      if (s->string_value) buffer_free(s->string_value);
      if (s->array_value) array_free(s->array_value);
      /* now we can free the plugin_config */
```

```
        free(s);
      }
      free(p->config_storage);
    }
    free(p);
    return HANDLER_GO_ON;
}

SETDEFAULTS_FUNC(mod_helloworld_set_defaults) {
  plugin_data *p = p_d;
  size_t i;
  config_values_t cv[] = {
    /* name, destination (set later), type, scope */
    {"our.fun", NULL, T_CONFIG_BOOLEAN, T_CONFIG_SCOPE_CONNECTION},
    {"our.port", NULL, T_CONFIG_SHORT, T_CONFIG_SCOPE_CONNECTION},
    {"our.number", NULL, T_CONFIG_INT, T_CONFIG_SCOPE_CONNECTION},
    {"we.love", NULL, T_CONFIG_STRING, T_CONFIG_SCOPE_CONNECTION},
    {"our.set", NULL, T_CONFIG_ARRAY, T_CONFIG_SCOPE_CONNECTION},
    {NULL, NULL, T_CONFIG_UNSET, T_CONFIG_SCOPE_UNSET}
    /* needs to end with a NULL entry */
  };
  if (!p) return HANDLER_ERROR;

  p->config_storage = calloc(1, srv->config_context->used *
      sizeof(specific_config *));
  for (i = 0; i < srv->config_context->used; i++) {
    plugin_config *s;
    s = calloc(1, sizeof(plugin_config));
    s->string_value = buffer_init();
    s->array_value = array_init();
    /* set the destinations to our new plugin_config */
    cv[0].destination = s->boolean_value;
    cv[1].destination = s->short_value;
    cv[2].destination = s->int_value;
    cv[3].destination = s->string_value;
    cv[4].destination = s->array_value;
    p->config_storage[i] = s;
    /* let Lighttpd do the rest */
    if (0 != config_insert_values_global(srv, ((data_config *)
        srv->config_context->data[i])->value, cv)) {
      return HANDLER_ERROR;
    }
  }
  return HANDLER_GO_ON;
}
```

If the configuration would be the same for all the pages, this would be all. However, Lighttpd allows us to carve out partitions of our site with different configuration rules using selectors. Each selector within the configuration file opens up a new context. We can use the `config_check_cond` function to see if the contents of the selector match. This is called a matched context.

Now, whenever we need to get the applicable configuration, we just run through all contexts. For each context, check if it matches, and if it does, put the contained entries into the `conf` entry of the `plugin` data. Note that the first context (with number zero) is the global context. This idiom is so common that almost every module has a function to do it, which is usually called `patch_connection`. Ours would look like this:

```
#define USED(n) (buffer_is_equal_string(du->key, CONST_STR_LEN(n)))
static int mod_helloworld_patch_connection(server *srv,
    connection *con, plugin_data *p) {
  size_t i, j;
  plugin_config *s = p->config_storage[0];
  /* default to global context, one PATCH_OPTION per option */
  PATCH_OPTION(boolean_value);
  PATCH_OPTION(short_value);
  PATCH_OPTION(int_value);
  PATCH_OPTION(string_value);
  PATCH_OPTION(array_value);
  /* Go through all contexts (but global) */
  for (i = 1; i < srv->config_context->used; i++) {
    data_config *dc = (data_config *)srv->config_context->data[i];
    s = p->config_storage[i];
    if (!config_check_cond(srv, con, dc)) continue;
    /* Got matching context, enter the given values */
   for (j = 0; j < dc->value->used; j++) {
      data_unset *du = dc->value->data[j];
      /* if the option was set in this context, use it */
      if (USED("our.fun")) PATCH_OPTION(boolean_value);
      if (USED("our.port")) PATCH_OPTION(short_value);
      if (USED("our.number")) PATCH_OPTION(int_value);
      if (USED("we.love")) PATCH_OPTION(string_value);
      if (USED("our.set")) PATCH_OPTION(array_value);
    }
  }
  return 0;
}
#undef USED
```

Now we can call this function from our handlers. After that, we can just use `p.conf` as the correct configuration for the context of this connection. Lighttpd defines the following handler callbacks (besides the `init`, `set_defaults`, and `cleanup` we have already used):

Plugin Callback Name	Called on Condition
handle_trigger	Every second (for example, cleaning cache, should be fast)
handle_sighup	On getting a sighup, it should re-read the configuration
handle_uri_raw	When the raw URI is in request.uri (for example, for rewrites)
handle_uri_clean	After the URI is URL-decoded (refer to `mod_access`)
handle_docroot	On getting the document root (refer to `mod_simple_vhost`)
handle_physical	Once the physical path has been set (refer to `mod_alias`)
handle_start_backend	Called after `handle_physical` if the file to serve exists
handle_send_request_content	Called to send out the request content
handle_response_header	Called to send out the response header
handle_filter_response_content	Called with the content, for example, for compression
handle_response_done	Called after the response is sent
connection_reset	Called after the request has been fully handled
handle_connection_close	Called when the connection is closed
handle_joblist	Called when all requests have been handled

The last two functions are marked as deprecated. However, `handle_connection_close` is still in use by `mod_proxy_core` and `mod_deflate` to clean up connection handling data. Maybe `handle_connection_close` will be merged with `connection_reset` in a later version of Lighttpd.

Rewriting the Request

As we can get the URL of our connection easily, it is a small step to change it. For example, we could want to add a random number to the filename to facilitate random image loading (apparently still quite a popular task). To make the task easy for us, we will add the number to the physical path after the URL has been parsed, not to disrupt the MIME type handling:

```
#include <stdlib.h>

#include "buffer.h"
#include "base.h"
#include "plugin.h"
```

```
#ifdef HAVE_CONFIG_H
#include "config.h"
#endif

typedef struct {
  unsigned int max;
} plugin_config;

typedef struct {
  PLUGIN_DATA;
  plugin_config **config_storage;
  plugin_config conf;
} plugin_data;

INIT_FUNC(mod_random_init) {
  plugin_data *p;
  UNUSED(srv);
  p = calloc(1, sizeof(*p));
  return p;
}

FREE_FUNC(mod_random_free) {
  plugin_data *p = p_d;
  UNUSED(srv);
  if (!p) return HANDLER_GO_ON;
  if (p->config_storage) {
    size_t i;
    for (i = 0; i < srv->config_context->used; i++) {
      plugin_config *s = p->config_storage[i];
      if (!s) continue;
      free(s);
    }
    free(p->config_storage);
  }
  free(p);
  return HANDLER_GO_ON;
}

SETDEFAULTS_FUNC(mod_random_set_defaults) {
  plugin_data *p = p_d;
  size_t i;
  config_values_t cv[] = {
    {"random.max", NULL, T_CONFIG_INT, T_CONFIG_SCOPE_CONNECTION},
    {NULL, NULL, T_CONFIG_UNSET, T_CONFIG_SCOPE_UNSET}
  };
  if (!p) return HANDLER_ERROR;
  p->config_storage = calloc(1, srv->config_context->used *
      sizeof(specific_config *));
```

```
    for (i = 0; i < srv->config_context->used; i++) {
      plugin_config *s;
      s = calloc(1, sizeof(plugin_config));
      cv[0].destination = s;
      p->config_storage[i] = s;
      if (0 != config_insert_values_global(srv, ((data_config *)
          srv->config_context->data[i])->value, cv)) {
        return HANDLER_ERROR;
      }
    }
  }
  return HANDLER_GO_ON;
}
static int mod_random_patch_connection(server *srv, connection *con,
    plugin_data *p) {
  size_t i, j;
  plugin_config *s = p->config_storage[0];
  PATCH_OPTION(max);
  for (i = 1; i < srv->config_context->used; i++) {
    data_config *dc = (data_config *)srv->config_context->data[i];
    s = p->config_storage[i];
    if (!config_check_cond(srv, con, dc)) continue;
    for (j = 0; j < dc->value->used; j++) {
      data_unset *du = dc->value->data[j];
      if (buffer_is_equal_string(du->key,
          CONST_STR_LEN("random.max"))) {
        PATCH_OPTION(max);
      }
    }
  }
  return 0;
}

URIHANDLER_FUNC(mod_random_uri_handler) {
  plugin_data *p = p_d;
  long r;
  UNUSED(srv);
  mod_random_patch_connection(srv, con, p);
  if (p->conf.max == 0) return HANDLER_GO_ON;
  /* get random value, shamelessly copied from "man rand" :-) */
  r = (long)((1.0 * p->conf.max) * (rand() / (RAND_MAX + 1.0)));
  buffer_append_long(con->physical.path, r);
  return HANDLER_GO_ON;
}

int mod_random_plugin_init(plugin *p) {
```

```
    p->version = LIGHTTPD_VERSION_ID;
    p->name = buffer_init_string("random");
    p->init = mod_random_init;
    p->handle_physical = mod_random_uri_handler;
    p->set_defaults = mod_random_set_defaults;
    p->cleanup = mod_random_free;
    p->data = NULL;
    return 0;
}
```

Compile and install again with the following commands (output omitted for brevity):

```
$ make mod_random.o
$ gcc -shared -o mod_random.so mod_random.o
$ /usr/bin/install -c mod_random.so /usr/local/lib/mod_random.so
```

This time we use a selector to limit the effect of mod_random. Add the following to our lighttpd.conf file:

```
server.modules = ("mod_random", ...)
$HTTP["url"] == "/image/ad.jpg" {
  random.max = 2
}
```

Now we should have three JPEG images in our image path related to the document root named "ad.jpg0", "ad.jpg1", and "ad.jpg2". If we browse to "image/ad.jpg", we will get served a random selection of those three images.

Note that we have already seen a more elegant and robust solution to this problem using mod_magnet in the last chapter.

Manipulating the Response

There are a few ways to change the response sent. We could change the header values with the handle_response_header callback, change where the response content comes from by using handle_read_response_content or change the response while it is sent out with the handle_filter_response_content callback.

Note that it is not absolutely necessary to use one of the callbacks to send out content. For example, mod_flv_streaming, which sends out the headers for an embedded flash video stream, does so by intercepting the handle_physical callback.

Writing a response is as easy as getting a buffer from the send `chunkqueue`, and then messing with the buffer contents. Some very useful functions to do this are defined in `buffer.h`. We could for example do the following:

```
/* Get output buffer */
buffer *out = chunkqueue_get_append_buffer(con->send);

/* Define some helpful variables */
buffer *some_other_buffer = get_some_buffer();
char *some_string = get_some_string();

/* Start out new with copy, then append */
BUFFER_COPY_STRING_CONST(out, "Hi there.\n");
buffer_append_string_buffer(out, some_other_buffer);
buffer_append_string(out, some_string);
buffer_append_string_len(out, some_string, 5); /* only char 0-4 */
buffer_append_long(123456789);
```

We also need to increase the number of bytes to send out by our buffer. Usually, we may also want to tell Lighttpd to close the connection to free valuable resources once we are finished.

```
con->send->bytes_in += out->used - 1; /* set bytes to send */
con->send->is_closed = 1; /* close the connection */
```

Another way is to put stuff directly onto the `chunkqueue`, which is shown with a few examples here:

```
#include "base.h"
#include "buffer.h"
#include "chunk.h"
/*  put a buffer onto the chunkqueue - will make a copy, so we keep
    responsibility for the memory. Good for writing data we do not
    own. */
chunkqueue_append_buffer(con->write_queue, con->request_uri.query);

/*  we can also put the buffer into the chunkqueue directly. This
    means the chunkqueue will take responsibility for freeing it so
    we don't need to. */
buffer *buffer = buffer_init();
buffer_append_memory(buffer, "Hello, World!", 13);
chunkqueue_append_buffer_weak(con->write_queue, buffer);

/* put a complete file onto the chunkqueue */
char *pathtofile = con->physical_path; /* in handle_physical_path */
int offset = 0; /* start from position zero */

int length; /* compute the length */
stat_cache_entry sce; /* defined in base.h */
```

```
int result = stat_cache_get_entry(srv, con, pathtofile, &sce);
if (HANDLER_ERROR == result) {
  con->http_status = 404; /* file not found */
    return HANDLER_FINISHED;
}
length = sce.st.st_size;

/* append the file from start to end onto the chunkqueue */
chunkqueue_append_file(con->write_queue, pathtofile, offset, length);
/* of course we can also use other values for offset and length */
return HANDLER_FINISHED;
```

The headers are stored as an array in the connection type. For example, we can add a X-We-Love=Lighttpd header with the following code:

```
/* get a data_string to put our header in */
data_string *ds = (data_string *)array_get_unused_element(
    con->response.headers, TYPE_STRING);
if (ds == NULL) ds = data_response_init();

/* set key and value and add our entry to the response headers */
BUFFER_COPY_STRING_CONST(ds->key, "X-We-Love");
BUFFER_COPY_STRING_CONST(ds->value, "Lighttpd");
array_insert_unique(con->response.headers, (data_unset *)ds);
```

The con->http_status field holds the HTTP status code that has already been shown for error handling. A list of status codes can be found in Appendix A. Finally, we can read the contents of files using the stream functions, which will give us a character pointer we can use for searching (refer to mod_ssi for example using PCRE):

```
stream s;
if (-1 == stream_open(&s, path)) {
  log_error_write(srv, __FILE__, __LINE__, "sb",
    "stream-open: ", path);
  return -1;
}
/* we can use s.start as a char *pointer to directly map the file. */
stream_close(&s);
```

The concluding example of this chapter is a workaround to the fact that many HTML pages do not declare a document type, which sends certain Internet browsers into the so-called "quirks mode", which means they will interpret layout information in a nonstandard way to be backwards-compatible to older versions that had the same faults.

Our `mod_doctype` takes two configuration strings, which will be put before `html` and `frameset` documents, respectively. The implementation is very basic, but with the right configuration, it might be useful nonetheless:

```
# put directly before mod_staticfile
server.modules = (..., "mod_doctype", "mod_staticfile" )
$HTTP["url"] =~ ".html$" {
  doctype.html = "<!DOCTYPE HTML PUBLIC \"-//W3C//DTD HTML 4.01\
    Transitional//EN\" \"http://www.w3.org/TR/html4/loose.dtd\">"
  doctype.frameset = "<!DOCTYPE HTML PUBLIC \"-//W3C//DTD HTML 4.01\
Frameset//EN\" \"http://www.w3.org/TR/html4/frameset.dtd\">
}
```

This tells `mod_doctype` to put the corresponding string as a document type declaration before the file contents. Without further ado, here is the code:

```
#include "log.h"
#include "stream.h"
#include "plugin.h"

/* First, we include needed header files and define our plugin_config
 * and data structure, as seen above.
 */
typedef struct {
  buffer *html_doctype;
  buffer *frameset_doctype;
} plugin_config;

typedef struct {
  PLUGIN_DATA;
  plugin_config **config_storage;
  plugin_config conf;
} plugin_data;

/* Our usual init function to claim the plugin data memory. */
INIT_FUNC(mod_doctype_init) {
  plugin_data *p;
  p = calloc(1, sizeof(*p));
  return p;
}

/* Helper function for mod_doctype_free, free a single plugin_config.
 */
void mod_doctype_freeconf(plugin_config *c) {
  if (!c) return; /* beware of the null value */
  if (c->html_doctype) buffer_free(c->html_doctype);
```

```
    if (c->frameset_doctype) buffer_free(c->frameset_doctype);
    free(c);
}

/* Our usual free function to let go of the memory for configuration.
*/
FREE_FUNC(mod_doctype_free) {
  plugin_data *p = p_d;
  UNUSED(srv);
  if (!p) return HANDLER_GO_ON;
  mod_doctype_freeconf(&(p->conf));
  if (p->config_storage) {
    size_t i; /* iterate over contexts, free plugin_configs */
    for (i = 0; i < srv->config_context->used; i++) {
      plugin_config *s = p->config_storage[i];
      mod_doctype_freeconf(s);
    }
    free(p->config_storage); /* free the storage array */
  }
  free(p); /* free our plugin_data struct */
  return HANDLER_GO_ON;
}

/* The set_defaults function also contains nothing surprising */
SETDEFAULTS_FUNC(mod_doctype_set_defaults) {
  plugin_data *p = p_d;
  size_t i;
  config_values_t cv[] = { /* name, destination, type, scope */
    {"doctype.html", NULL, T_CONFIG_STRING,
      T_CONFIG_SCOPE_CONNECTION},
    {"doctype.frameset", NULL, T_CONFIG_STRING,
      T_CONFIG_SCOPE_CONNECTION},
    {NULL, NULL, T_CONFIG_UNSET, T_CONFIG_SCOPE_UNSET}
  };
  if (!p) return HANDLER_ERROR;

  p->config_storage = calloc(1, srv->config_context->used *
      sizeof(specific_config *));
  for (i = 0; i < srv->config_context->used; i++) {
    plugin_config *s;
    s = calloc(1, sizeof(plugin_config));
    s->html_doctype = buffer_init();
    s->frameset_doctype = buffer_init();
    cv[0].destination = s->html_doctype;
    cv[1].destination = s->frameset_doctype;
```

```
      p->config_storage[i] = s;
      if (0 != config_insert_values_global(srv, ((data_config *)
          srv->config_context->data[i])->value, cv)) {
        return HANDLER_ERROR;
      }
    }
    return HANDLER_GO_ON;
}


/* The usual patch_connection function - nothing new here
 */
#define PATCH(x) p->conf.x = s->x;
static int mod_doctype_patch_connection(server *srv, connection *con,
      plugin_data *p) {
  size_t i, j;
  plugin_config *s = p->config_storage[0];
  PATCH(html_doctype);
  PATCH(frameset_doctype);
  for (i = 1; i < srv->config_context->used; i++) {
    data_config *dc = (data_config *)srv->config_context->data[i];
    s = p->config_storage[i];
    if (!config_check_cond(srv, con, dc)) continue;
    for (j = 0; j < dc->value->used; j++) { /* get all values */
      data_unset *du = dc->value->data[j];
      if (buffer_is_equal_string(du->key,
          CONST_STR_LEN("doctype.html"))) {
        PATCH(html_doctype); /* set html_doctype, if found */
      } else if (buffer_is_equal_string(du->key,
          CONST_STR_LEN("doctype.frameset"))) {
        PATCH(frameset_doctype); /* set frameset_doctype */
      }
    }
  }
  return 0;
}
#undef PATCH

/* A helper function to determine if a html file contains a frameset.
 * Uses a stream to peek at the file contents.
 */
static int mod_doctype_is_frameset(server *srv, buffer *path) {
  stream s;
  int result;
  if (-1 == stream_open(&s, path)) {
```

```
        log_error_write(srv, __FILE__, __LINE__, "sb", "stream-open: ",
          path);
        return 0; /* defaulting to no frameset */
    }
    result = !strstr("<frameset", s.start); /* search for frameset */
    stream_close(&s); /* close the stream, release resources */
    return result;
}

/* Our physical path handling function.
 */
URIHANDLER_FUNC(mod_doctype_physical_path) {
    plugin_data *p = p_d;
    size_t i;
    if (con->physical.path->used == 0) return HANDLER_GO_ON;
    mod_doctype_patch_connection(srv, con, p);
    for (i = 0; i < p->conf.html_doctype->used; i++) {
        data_string *ds = (data_string *)p->conf.html_doctype;
        buffer *doctype;
        if (ds->value->used == 0) continue;
        if (mod_doctype_is_frameset(srv, con->physical.path)) {
            doctype = p->conf.frameset_doctype;
        } else {
            doctype = p->conf.html_doctype;
        }
        chunkqueue_append_buffer(con->write_queue, doctype);
        return HANDLER_GO_ON; /* let mod_staticfile do the rest */
    }
    return HANDLER_GO_ON;
}

/* Here is our basic init function. No surprise here, either.
 */
int mod_doctype_plugin_init(plugin *p) {
    p->version = LIGHTTPD_VERSION_ID;
    p->name = buffer_init_string("doctype");

    p->init = mod_doctype_init;
    p->handle_subrequest_start = mod_doctype_physical_path;
    p->set_defaults = mod_doctype_set_defaults;
    p->cleanup = mod_doctype_free;
    p->data = NULL;
    return 0;
}
```

Note that the module does not allow for HTTP range requests, because adding this would have diverted from the basics of handling streams, buffers, and the write queue. The mod_doctype_physical_path function looks at the configuration context to see if our document type adding applies, and then uses the mod_doctype_is_ frameset function to decide which document type string to use. It then adds the selected buffer to the write queue and hands it over to mod_staticfile, which will then send out the file. For the record, this is a 140 line C program where a 14 line mod_magnet script (even with short lines) would have done the job, with none of the restrictions of the C code:

```lua
# mod_doctype.lua
local p = lighty.env["physical.doc-root"] + lighty.env["request.uri"]
local f = io.open(p, "r")
if f:read("*a"):find("<frameset", 0, true) then
  lighty.content = {'<!DOCTYPE HTML PUBLIC "-//W3C//DTD HTML 4.01\
Transitional//EN" "http://www.w3.org/TR/html4/loose.dtd">',
{filename=path}}
else
  lighty.content = {'<!DOCTYPE HTML PUBLIC "-//W3C//DTD HTML 4.01\
Frameset//EN" "http://www.w3.org/TR/html4/frameset.dtd">',
{filename=path}}
end
f:close()
return 200
```

This is a good example of why we should think twice before writing a module. The probability of errors is directly proportional to the number of code lines. So we are bound to get ten times as many errors in the C module. Moreover, the mod_magnet script is easier to put to use.

Nevertheless, if we have a compelling need (and looking from the modules section on the Lighttpd wiki, people do find good uses for new modules), a module can fill a niche where a mod_magnet script will be too slow, high-level or resource intensive. And finally there are libraries that do not have Lua bindings, so we are left with the choice of writing a Lighttpd module or a Lua binding.

Summary

As we have seen, writing modules, while not exactly easy, is certainly doable for an average C programmer. Lighttpd goes out of its way to make its plugin API powerful and simple to use. But before writing a plugin, we should ask ourselves a few questions:

- Is the solution from outside of Lighttpd sensible?
- Does the Lighttpd core or a standard module do the job?
- Can I write a `mod_magnet` script to solve my problem?
- Which standard module is the easiest to extend to solve the problem?

Only if we answer the first three questions with "no", we should consider writing a module. The fourth question gives us a hint if we should extend another module that solves a similar problem (be sure to read the license in COPYING first) or start from `mod_skeleton.c`, which is supplied with the Lighttpd source. Alternatively, feel free to use any of the implementations given in this chapter as a starting point. Oh, and if the result is a useful plugin, think about giving it back to the Lighttpd community. Thanks!

A
HTTP Status Codes

Code	Used For / Meaning
100 Continue	These codes are reserved for future versions
101 Switching Protocols	
200 OK	The usual response to a GET
201 Created	The correct response to a PUT/POST
202 Accepted	The server accepted the data, but did not do anything with it yet (for example in case of an upload)
203 Non-Authoritative Information	Usually sent by a proxy
204 No Content	This is a good way to tell a client the page has not been updated
205 Reset Content	This tells the client to reset all form fields
206 Partial Content	This is implemented in HTTP 1.1 as a response for a range request
300 Multiple Choice	Give the client a choice where to fetch the data, for example, for mirrors
301 Moved Permanently	Tell the browser to redirect and update bookmarks
302 Moved Temporarily	Tell the browser to redirect for now. Refer to Chapter 2 for further information.
303 See other	Redirects a POST request to a GET request.
304 Not modified	Means the same as 204, but answers an If-Modified request
305 Use Proxy	Tells the client to connect through a proxy server
307 Temporary Redirect	Sent if a client denies a 302

Code	Used For / Meaning
400 Bad Request	The request does not conform to the HTTP syntax
401 Access Denied	Sent by mod_auth; initiates HTTP authorization. Refer to Chapter 7 for further information
402 Payment required	For micropayment (not implemented)
403 Forbidden	If the server could not access a file or if the HTTP authorization failed
404 Not found	The file was not found on the server. Refer to `server.error-handler-404` in Chapter 2.
405 Method not allowed	The client should try a different method
406 Not Acceptable	The request was denied for formal reasons
407 Proxy Authentication required	A HTTP proxy should be used for authenticating the client
408 Timeout	Self descriptive, isn't it? Refer to `server.timeout` in Chapter 2
409 Conflict	A file to read/write is locked.
410 Gone	The page has moved to an unknown location, so a redirect is not possible.
411 Length Required	The server requires a Content-Length header on POST request
412 Precondition Failed	A Precondition specified in the request could not be satisfied
413 Request Entity Too Large	Some of the request entities were too large to fit in the buffers; Bad luck.
414 Request URL Too Long	The URL did not fit in the buffer so the request was probably bad anyway.
415 Unsupported Media Type	The client asked a MIME type that the server did not know
416 Request Range Not Satisfiable	We got a HTTP 1.1 range request with a negative or overflowing range
417 Expectation Failed	The client sent an Expect header with the request, but we could not fulfill it
500 Internal Server Error	Usually the result of a CGI script gone wrong
501 Not Implemented	Sent out for a non-HTTP1.1 request—anything but GET, HEAD, or POST
502 Bad Gateway	Another server on the backend returned an error
503 Service Unavailable	There was an error on the backend site, but it will be fixed real soon now
504 Gateway Timeout	The request was proxied to another server, but the proxied request timed out
505 HTTP Version Not Supported	Lighttpd will send this for any version above 1.1

B
Module/Configuration Index

Internal

 Here ☑ stands for a switch with the possible values "enable" and "disable", 123 stands for a number, ABC stands for a string, (...) stands for a list and (X=>Y) for a mapping of values.

Name	Type	Description
connection.kbytes-per-second	123	Throttle the traffic per connection
debug.log-condition-cache-handling	☑	Enable debug logging for different parts of the Lighttpd server
debug.log-condition-handling	☑	
debug.log-file-not-found	☑	
debug.log-request-handling	☑	
debug.log-request-header	☑	
debug.log-request-header-on-error	☑	
debug.log-response-header	☑	
debug.log-state-handling	☑	
debug.log-timing	☑	Enable timing information in log messages
mimetype.assign	(X=>Y)	Assign a mimetype to file extensions
mimetype.use-xattr	☑	Use the xattr call to get the mime type if we use the X File System.
server.bind	ABC	Binds Lighttpd to the specified hostname. Otherwise the request hostname is used.

Name	Type	Description
server.chroot	ABC	The directory to chroot into
server.core-files	☑	Enable Resource Limiting for core files
server.docroot	OLD	Use server.document-root instead
server.document-root	ABC	The main directory where Lighttpd gets the files from
server.error-handler-404	ABC	Path to a file to serve on File not Found
server.errorfile-prefix	ABC	Path/prefix (+ error-code + ".html") to file
server.errorlog	ABC	Path to a file where errors are logged
server.errorlog-use-syslog	☑	Alternatively use syslog for error logging
server.event-handler	ABC	Event handler to use (refer to Chapter 9)
server.follow-symlink	☑	Enable Lighttpd following symbolic links
server.force-lower-case-files	OLD	Use server.force-lowercase-filenames instead
server.force-lowercase-filenames	☑	Force all filenames to lower case
server.groupid	OLD	Use server.groupname instead
server.groupname	ABC	Run Lighttpd with this group
server.host	OLD	Use server.bind instead
server.kbytes-per-second	123	Throttle the server-wide throughput
server.max-connection-idle	123	Limit the number of idle connections
server.max-connections	123	Limit the number of overall connections
server.max-fds	123	Limit the number of file descriptors
server.max-keep-alive-idle	123	Seconds before an idle keepalive session is dropped
server.max-keep-alive-requests	123	Number of requests before a keepalive session is dropped
server.max-read-idle	123	Timeout for receiving data
server.max-read-threads	123	Limit the number of threads for read calls
server.max-request-size	123	Limit the request size until a 413 is sent
server.max-stat-threads	123	Limit the number of threads for stat calls
server.max-worker	123	Limit the number of worker processes (for multi-CPU) to spawn.
server.max-write-idle	123	Timeout for sending data
server.modules	(...)	Which modules to use
server.name	ABC	The Server Name, defaults to hostname

Name	Type	Description
server.network-backend	ABC	Backend to use (refer to Chapter 9)
server.pid-file	ABC	A file to store Lighttpds pid (for example, for init)
server.port	123	The port to bind to; or use selectors
server.protocol-http11	☑	Enable HTTP1.1 (usually enabled)
server.range-requests	☑	Allow serving the specific ranges of files
server.stat-cache-engine	ABC	"disable", "simple", or "fam" (if available)
server.tag	ABC	Set the server tag (defaults to Lighttpd + version)
server.upload-dirs	(...)	Set the directories for file upload
server.use-ipv6	☑	Enable IPv6 connections
server.use-keep-alive	OLD	Use server.max-keep-alive-requests = 0 to disable keep-alive instead
server.use-noatime	☑	Disable setting access time on read
server.userid	OLD	Use server.username instead
server.username	ABC	Run Lighttpd with this user
server.virtual-default-host	OLD	Load mod_simple_vhost and use simple-vhost.default-host instead
server.virtual-docroot	OLD	Stricken since 1.5.0.
server.virtual-root	OLD	A list of ciphers, default is now TLS
ssl.ca-file	ABC	Enable SSL
ssl.cipher-list	(...)	Path to the certificate file, See Chapter 8
ssl.engine	☑	Stricken since 1.5.0, default is now TLS
ssl.pemfile	ABC	
ssl.use-sslv2	☑	

mod_access

Name	Type	Description
access.deny-all	☑	Since 1.5.0, denies access to all files; usually set within a selector.
url.access-deny	(...)	Denies access to matching files

mod_accesslog

Name	Type	Description
accesslog.filename	ABC	Path to a file for log requests
accesslog.format	ABC	A template string, refer to Chapter 7
accesslog.use-syslog	☑	Use syslog instead of logging to file

mod_alias

Name	Type	Description
alias.url	(X=>Y)	Map URLs to document roots

mod_auth

Name	Type	Description
auth.backend	ABC	"plain", "htpasswd", "htdigest", or "ldap"
auth.backend.htdigest.userfile	ABC	Path to htdigest userfile
auth.backend.htpasswd.userfile	ABC	Path to htpasswd userfile
auth.backend.ldap.allow-empty-pw	☑	Since 1.5.0, allows bind with no password
auth.backend.ldap.base-dn	ABC	The base dn of the LDAP directory
auth.backend.ldap.bind-dn	ABC	The user dn with which to bind
auth.backend.ldap.bind-pw	ABC	The password for binding
auth.backend.ldap.ca-file	ABC	A certificate authority file. Refer to Chapter 6.
auth.backend.ldap.cert	ABC	Since 1.5.0, the public certificate (for self-signing)
auth.backend.ldap.filter	ABC	A search filter for LDAP accounts
auth.backend.ldap.hostname	ABC	The LDAP directory server (IP address)
auth.backend.ldap.key	ABC	Since 1.5.0, the private key for self-signing, use in conjunction with auth.backend.ldap.cert.
auth.backend.ldap.starttls	☑	Enables Secure LDAP over TLS
auth.backend.plain.groupfile	ABC	Path to a plain groupfile (user:group)
auth.backend.plain.userfile	ABC	Path to a plain userfile (user:password)
auth.debug	123	Sets the debug level for this module
auth.require	(X=>Y)	Maps matching URLs to requirements (Refer to Chapter 7)

mod_cgi

Name	Type	Description
cgi.assign	(...)	Map matching URLs to CGI processes; refer to Chapter 3, 10, and 12
cgi.execute-all	☑	Since 1.5.0

mod_cml

This module has been introduced in version 1.3.15 and was replaced by the more powerful mod_magnet (see below) in version 1.4.12.

Name	Type	Description
cml.extension	ABC	Lighty will interpret all the files ending with this string by mod_cml, for example, "cml"
cml.memcache-hosts	(...)	A list of memcached hosts
cml.memcache-namespace	ABC	Memcached namespace of the cache
cml.power-magnet	ABC	Since 1.4.9, mod_cml can intercept all requests to a single Lua file by setting power-magnet to the name of the file

mod_chunked

This module was introduced in version 1.5.0 to allow for chunked encoding of traffic.

Name	Type	Description
chunked.debug	123	Sets the debug level for this module
chunked.encoding	☑	Enables chunked encoding

mod_compress

Name	Type	Description
compress.cache-dir	ABC	Path to a directory used for caching
compress.filetype	(...)	A list of file extensions to compress
compress.max-filesize	123	Compresses files to the given size

mod_deflate

This module is a modified version of `mod_compress` and was introduced in 1.5.0 to allow compression of dynamic content.

Name	Type	Description
deflate.allowed_encodings	(...)	Since 1.5.0, one to three of ("bzip2", "gzip", "deflate")
deflate.compression-level	123	Compression level for bzip2 algorithm (1..9)
deflate.debug	☑	Enables Debugging for this module
deflate.enabled	☑	Enables deflate compression
deflate.mem-level	123	Memory level for deflate compression (1..9)
deflate.mimetypes	(...)	Deflates the given mime types
deflate.min-compress-size	123	Minimum size a file must be compressed to
deflate.output-buffer-size	123	Set the output buffer size in bytes
deflate.sync-flush	☑	Enable to send output to the browser while compressing the rest
deflate.window-size	123	For gzip compression the window size is two to the power of this value (8..15)
deflate.work-block-size	123	The number of bytes to compress at once

mod_dirlisting

Name	Type	Description
dir-listing.activate	☑	Enables directory listings
dir-listing.encoding	ABC	Character encoding to use (for example, UTF-8)
dir-listing.exclude	(...)	Omits listing the matching directories
dir-listing.external-css	ABC	Path to the external CSS file to be included
dir-listing.hide-dotfiles	☑	Hides files starting with dot in the list
dir-listing.hide-header-file	☑	Hides `HEADER.txt` from the list
dir-listing.hide-readme-file	☑	Hides the README.txt file, if it exists
dir-listing.show-header	☑	Shows the contents of the HEADER.txt before listing the directory
dir-listing.show-readme	☑	Shows the contents of README.txt before listing the directory
server.dir-listing	☑	Globally enables/disables directory listing

mod_evasive

Name	Type	Description
evasive.max-conns-per-ip	123	Limits open connections per IP

mod_evhost

Name	Type	Description
evhost.path-pattern	ABC	A template for the path; refer to Chapter 3

mod_expire

Name	Type	Description
expire.url	(X=>Y)	Expires matching URIs after a given interval from access or modification. The interval is given as a number plus a unit where the unit is in seconds, minutes, hours, days, weeks, months, or years

mod_fastcgi

In version 1.5.0, `mod_fastcgi` has been deprecated and replaced by `mod_proxy_core` and `mod_proxy_backend_fastcgi`.

Name	Type	Description
fastcgi.debug	123	Sets the debug level for this module
fastcgi.map-extensions	(...)	Maps file extensions to script interpreters
fastcgi.server	(X=>Y)	Maps matching URIs to FastCGI server processes; see Chapter 3

mod_flv_streaming

Name	Type	Description
flv-streaming.extensions	(...)	A list of extensions to stream (usually flv)

mod_indexfile

Name	Type	Description
index-file.names	(...)	Uses the first file found in the list as index
server.indexfiles	(...)	The same as `index-file.names`

mod_magnet

`mod_magnet` embeds the scripting language Lua into Lighttpd to mess with the request-response chain. For further information refer to Chapter 12.

Name	Type	Description
magnet.attract-physical	(X=>Y)	= attract-physical-path-to in version 1.5.0
magnet.attract-physical-path-to	(X=>Y)	Maps encountered paths to Lua files
magnet.attract-raw	(X=>Y)	= attract-raw-url-to in version 1.5.0
magnet.attract-raw-url-to	(X=>Y)	Maps encountered URLs to Lua files
magnet.attract-response-content-to	(X=>Y)	Mangle the content after the headers have been sent
magnet.attract-response-header-to	(X=>Y)	Mangle only the headers

mod_proxy

This module has been replaced in version 1.5.0 by `mod_proxy_core` and `mod_proxy_backend_http`.

Name	Type	Description
proxy.balance	ABC	Selects the proxy algorithm from "hash", "round-robin" or "fair"
proxy.debug	123	Sets the debug level for this module
proxy.server	(X=>Y)	Maps matching URLs to HTTP servers

mod_proxy_core

Since version 1.5.0, `mod_proxy_core` replaces `mod_proxy`, and the various `mod_*cgis`. We still need to load the backend modules for using them (starting with `mod_proxy_backend_`, followed by the protocol name, see `proxy-core.protocol`).

Name	Type	Description
proxy-core.allow-x-rewrite	☑	Enables X-Rewrite headers to relay request to another host
proxy-core.allow-x-sendfile	☑	Enables X-Sendfile headers to send an already created file
proxy-core.backends	(...)	A list of hosts, either as IP addresses, hostnames or UNIX sockets
proxy-core.balancer	ABC	Selects the load-balancing algorithm (one of "round-robin", "sqf", "carp" or "static")
proxy-core.check-local	OLD	This was a workaround to a PHP bug, but should no longer be necessary
proxy-core.debug	123	Sets the debug level for this module
proxy-core.max-keep-alive-requests	123	Requests until keep-alive session closes
proxy-core.max-pool-size	123	Size of the connection pool per backend
proxy-core.protocol	ABC	Selects the protocol to use ('http', 'fastcgi', 'ajp13', or 'scgi')
proxy-core.rewrite-request	(X=>Y)	Rewrites request headers or URI (similar to mod_rewrite, but works on other request parameters: "_uri", "_docroot", "_pathinfo", "_scriptname"
proxy-core.rewrite-response	(X=>Y)	Rewrites response headers (by name);
proxy-core.split-hostnames	☑	Disabling this option allows pooling addresses if there are multiple IP addresses for a given DNS hostname

mod_redirect

Name	Type	Description
url.redirect	(X=>Y)	Matching URLs are redirected, see Chapter 2
url.redirect-code	123	Since 1.5.0, this tells Lighttpd which redirect code to use (refer to Appendix A)

mod_rewrite

Name	Type	Description
url.rewrite	(X=>Y)	= url.rewrite-once
url.rewrite-final	(X=>Y)	= url.rewrite-once
url.rewrite-once	(X=>Y)	Maps search patterns to replacement templates, will be executed once.
url.rewrite-repeat	(X=>Y)	Same as rewrite-once, but will be executed until the pattern no longer matches (at most a 100 times).

mod_rrdtool

mod_rrdtool might be stricken from 1.5.0 until the final release, leaving mod_status to fill the niche, as Jan Kneschke has hinted in the Lighttpd blog. However, the pre-releases so far still have it. Refer to Chapter 7 for instructions on how to setup Lighttpd with rrdtool.

Name	Type	Description
rrdtool.binary	ABC	Path to the rrdtool binary
rrdtool.db-name	ABC	Path to the rrdtool database

mod_scgi

This module has been replaced in version 1.5.0 by mod_proxy_core and mod_proxy_backend_scgi.

Name	Type	Description
scgi.debug	123	Sets debug level for this module
scgi.server	(X=>Y)	Maps matching URIs to SCGI processes; see Chapter 3

mod_secure_download

A way of securing downloads by an application supplied token, which is generated with a timestamp and invalidated after a given time. Refer to Chapter 4 for further information.

Name	Type	Description
secdownload.document-root	ABC	Document-root of the download area
secdownload.secret	ABC	A "secret" which will be hashed into a token together with a timestamp
secdownload.timeout	123	Seconds until the token is invalidated
secdownload.uri-prefix	ABC	The download URL will consist of this prefix, the token and the path to the file to download

mod_setenv

`mod_setenv` manipulates the environment, request, or response headers for external processes. The configuration statements are best used within selectors. Refer to Chapter 5 for further information.

Name	Type	Description
setenv.add-environment	(X=>Y)	Key-Value map to add to environment
setenv.add-request-header	(X=>Y)	Key-Value map to add to HTTP request headers
setenv.add-response-header	(X=>Y)	Key-Value map to add to HTTP response headers

mod_simple_vhost

Name	Type	Description
simple-vhost.debug	123	Sets the debug level for this module
simple-vhost.default-host	ABC	Defaults to this host on missing directory
simple-vhost.document-root	ABC	The path is created by appending the server-root, the hostname, and the document-root
simple-vhost.server-root	ABC	

mod_sql_vhost_core, mod_mysql_vhost

Before 1.5.0, mod_mysql_vhost was self-contained. In 1.5.0, the non-MySQL-specific parts have been pulled into mod_sql_vhost_core, so there may be more database backends in the future. In 1.5.0, the server.modules needs both entries in the above order. Refer to Chapter 3 for more information.

Name	Type	Description
mysql-vhost.db	ABC	mod_mysql_vhost as *user* using *pass* as
mysql-vhost.hostname	ABC	password will connect to *hostname:port*,
mysql-vhost.pass	ABC	uses the *db* database and executes the *sql* statement which has a ? as placeholder for
mysql-vhost.port	123	the hostname
mysql-vhost.sock	ABC	(italic words are directives, to be prefixed
mysql-vhost.sql	ABC	with mysql-vhost)
mysql-vhost.user	ABC	
sql-vhost.backend	ABC	The backend (only "mysql" for now)
sql-vhost.cache-ttl	123	The Cache Time-to-live in seconds
sql-vhost.db	ABC	The new mysql-vhost.db
sql-vhost.debug	123	Sets the debug level for this module
sql-vhost.hostname	ABC	The new mysql-vhost.hostname
sql-vhost.pass	ABC	The new mysql-vhost.pass
sql-vhost.port	123	The new mysql-vhost.port
sql-vhost.select-vhost	ABC	The new mysql-vhost.sql
sql-vhost.sock	ABC	A socket for a local database server
sql-vhost.user	ABC	The new mysql-vhost.user

mod_ssi

Name	Type	Description
ssi.extension	(...)	List of file extensions for which to use Server Side Includes

mod_staticfile

Name	Type	Description
static-file.exclude-extensions	(...)	List of file extensions for which to forbid static access (for example, ("php") to secure against serving source code)

mod_status

mod_status displays the status, statistics and configuration information about the running server. Usually, we want to protect the configured URLs with mod_auth (see above).

Name	Type	Description
status.config-url	ABC	The URL to display the configuration
status.enable-sort	☑	Enables client-side javascript sorting for the statistics page
status.statistics-url	ABC	The URL for the statistics page
status.status-url	ABC	The URL for the status page

mod_trigger_b4_dl

This module protects a download by a trigger site which must be visited before. Refer to Chapter 4 for further information.

Name	Type	Description
trigger-before-download.debug	☑	Enables debugging for this module
trigger-before-download.deny-url	ABC	The URL where untriggered downloads will end up
trigger-before-download.download-url	ABC	The download URL to protect
trigger-before-download.gdbm-filename	ABC	Stores triggers in a local gdbm database
trigger-before-download.memcache-hosts	(...)	A list of memcached hosts to store triggers externally
trigger-before-download.memcache-namespace	ABC	The namespace for triggers
trigger-before-download.trigger-timeout	123	Seconds to trigger deletion
trigger-before-download.trigger-url	ABC	The URL that triggers a valid access

mod_uploadprogress

Returns the status of running uploads as JSON containing three entries: state (one of starting, error, done, uploading), status (the HTML status), size (total bytes), received (bytes received so far).

Name	Type	Description
upload-progress.debug	☑	Enables debug messages for this module
upload-progress.progress-url	ABC	If set, activates progress information on this URL
upload-progress.remove-timeout	123	Time in seconds until connections are no longer tracked (defaults to 60)

mod_userdir

Name	Type	Description
userdir.basepath	ABC	The prefix of all userdirs, for example "/users/"
userdir.exclude-user	(...)	A list of users to exclude from userdir
userdir.include-user	(...)	Alternatively, userdir can be limited to a list of users
userdir.path	ABC	The suffix after the username, for example "public_html"

mod_usertrack

Refer to Chapter 5 for further information

Name	Type	Description
usertrack.cookie-domain	ABC	The domain of the tracking cookie (usually your hostname)
usertrack.cookie-max-age	123	Seconds of user inactivity until the cookie is invalidated
usertrack.cookie-name	ABC	The name of the tracking cookie
usertrack.cookiename	OLD	Use usertrack.cookie-name instead

mod_webdav

Name	Type	Description
webdav.activate	☑	Activate webdav, usually within selector
webdav.is-readonly	☑	If set, disables writing to the webdav folder
webdav.log-xml	☑	Path to an XML file to log on
webdav.sqlite-db-name	ABC	Name of a SQLite database in which to store locks. Note that locking has to be enabled at installation

Index

**Thank you for buying
Lighttpd**

Packt Open Source Project Royalties

When we sell a book written on an Open Source project, we pay a royalty directly to that project. Therefore by purchasing Lighttpd, Packt will have given some of the money received to the Lighttpd project.

In the long term, we see ourselves and you — customers and readers of our books — as part of the Open Source ecosystem, providing sustainable revenue for the projects we publish on. Our aim at Packt is to establish publishing royalties as an essential part of the service and support a business model that sustains Open Source.

If you're working with an Open Source project that you would like us to publish on, and subsequently pay royalties to, please get in touch with us.

Writing for Packt

We welcome all inquiries from people who are interested in authoring. Book proposals should be sent to author@packtpub.com. If your book idea is still at an early stage and you would like to discuss it first before writing a formal book proposal, contact us; one of our commissioning editors will get in touch with you.

We're not just looking for published authors; if you have strong technical skills but no writing experience, our experienced editors can help you develop a writing career, or simply get some additional reward for your expertise.

About Packt Publishing

Packt, pronounced 'packed', published its first book "Mastering phpMyAdmin for Effective MySQL Management" in April 2004 and subsequently continued to specialize in publishing highly focused books on specific technologies and solutions.

Our books and publications share the experiences of your fellow IT professionals in adapting and customizing today's systems, applications, and frameworks. Our solution-based books give you the knowledge and power to customize the software and technologies you're using to get the job done. Packt books are more specific and less general than the IT books you have seen in the past. Our unique business model allows us to bring you more focused information, giving you more of what you need to know, and less of what you don't.

Packt is a modern, yet unique publishing company, which focuses on producing quality, cutting-edge books for communities of developers, administrators, and newbies alike. For more information, please visit our website: www.PacktPub.com.

Xen Virtualization

ISBN: 978-1-847192-48-6 Paperback: 150 pages

A fast and practical guide to supporting multiple operating systems with the Xen hypervisor

1. Installing and configuring Xen

2. Managing and administering Xen servers and virtual machines

3. Setting up networking, storage, and encryption

4. Backup and migration

Hacking Vim

ISBN: 978-1-847190-93-2 Paperback: 228 pages

From personalizing Vim to productivity optimizations: Recipes to make life easier for experienced Vim users

1. Create, install, and use Vim scripts

2. Personalize your work-area

3. Optimize your Vim editor to be faster and more responsive

Please check **www.PacktPub.com** for information on our titles

www.ingramcontent.com/pod-product-compliance
Lightning Source LLC
Chambersburg PA
CBHW060546060326
40690CB00017B/3620